# NATURAL AREAS OF THE SAN JUAN ISLANDS

*Terry Domico*

*

*Cartography by Eleana Pawl*

**Turtleback Books**
Friday Harbor, Washington

# NATURAL AREAS OF THE SAN JUAN ISLANDS

Copyright 2007 by Turtleback Books
Photographs and text by Terry Domico
Cartography by Eleana Pawl

*Turtleback Books, Post Office Box 2012,*
*Friday Harbor, Washington 98250 USA*

## For Ordering Information

Please contact Turtleback Books at (360) 378-3105
E-mail: turtlebackbooks@usa.com
Quantity purchase discounts are available.

## Visit our website at: www.turtlebackbooks.net

---

Domico, Terry (1946-  )
    Natural Areas of the San Juan Islands / Terry Domico;
    Cartography by Eleana Pawl
    Includes bibiological references, glossary, and index.

    ISBN: 978-1-883385-28-6

    Library of Congress Control Number: 2006936435

1. Natural history-Washington (State)-San Juan Islands.  2. Natural history-British Columbia-Haro Strait  3. Terrestrial habitats-Washington (State)-San Juan Islands. 4. Terrestrial habitats-British Columbia-Haro Strait.  5. Nearshore environments-Washington (State)-San Juan Islands. 6. Nearshore environments-British Columbia -Haro Strait.

Printed in the United States of America.

10 9 8 7 6 5 4 3 2 1

# NATURAL AREAS
# OF THE
# SAN JUAN ISLANDS

## Terry Domico

\*

*Cartography by Eleana Pawl*

To the stewards of our lands...
and all who appreciate our
natural heritage.

*

*

Other Fine Books by
Internationally Acclaimed
Nature Writer and Photographer
Terry Domico

*Wild Harvest*

*Bears of the World*

*Kangaroos: The Marvelous Mob*

*The Nature of Borneo* (Photography)

*The Last Thylacine*

*

# CONTENTS

# INTRODUCTION

The inspiration for this book occurred to me more than twenty years ago. It was to be a book about the "special" areas in the San Juan Islands where bird watchers and botanists could go and enjoy their "naturalist arts" in relative solitude. In fact, for several years I made notes and site assessments for just such a book. But the idea of calling public attention to these incredibly beautiful and highly biodiverse places in my beloved islands was more than I could bear. I did not want to see my favorite places being overwhelmed and trampled by uncaring visitors who scattered litter about and let their dogs chase the local wildlife. Although I continued my explorations and assessments of the "hidden" places in the islands, I let the book project gradually slip away.

Then an event happened that completely changed my thinking on this subject... a paradigm shift if you will. It occurred one summer while bird specialist Kanda Kumar and I were camped on Jones Island. During the long daylight hours, we occupied ourselves with bird watching and by conducting habitat assessments in the nearby "outer" islands, using a motorboat that we could safely beach whenever we wished.

One day we stopped on Gossip Island, located in the mouth of Stuart Island's Reid Harbor. It is a teeny little island - barely two and a half acres at low tide - but the biological community that we discovered there surprised us. Among other animals, we saw a family of river otter and a black-tailed deer that dashed into the water and swam off to the main island upon our arrival. We also spotted a pair of nesting black oyster-catchers (a distinctive shorebird) and several recently fledged fox sparrows with their attentive parents. More importantly, we found an intact remnant community of Puget Sound native prairie. All of the forbs and wildflower indicator plants were present ... and there on a rocky bald was the largest colony of narrow-leaved sedum (*Sedum lanceolatum*) that we had ever seen. (This regionally endemic species is waning in western Washington and we had been asked by at least two botanists to keep an eye out for it.)

Later that day, as we reviewed our notes back in camp, we noticed the State Parks patrol boat *Sea Bass* coming into Jones Island's north bay and approaching the dock. Out of the boat stepped Dave Castor, area manager for several of the State Marine Parks including Jones Island. The other man who stepped onto the dock wore a business suit. This was interesting.

Both of them came over to our little research camp to say "Hello." We offered them a beer. The gentleman in the suit and tie was introduced as a State Parks Commissioner. Even more interesting.

"How's it going?" Dave asked us.

"Gossip Island!" Kanda and I both blurted. Then we excitedly described the wonderful biodiversity that we had found.

As we talked, I noticed that both men began to wear "long" faces.
"What's wrong?" I asked.
"Well, you know that Gossip is State Land?" Dave began carefully.
"Yes...," I answered suspiciously.
"Well... We're planning to develop some permanent campsites on that island," the Commissioner explained. "The materials have already been ordered."
"What?!!" we cried. "The sedum and the little prairie are liable to be trampled and lost."
"Isn't there anything we can do?" I asked the Commissioner.
"You could petition the State Parks Commission in Olympia for a review," he suggested. "It might help."

After the men had left to go back to their boat, Kanda and I decided to break camp and return to Friday Harbor the next morning. We moved into my little office on Court Street (this became our campaign headquarters), and during the next few days we contacted the local newspapers, the Washington Native Plant Society, the Audubon Society, and the Washington Water Trails Association to notify them of what would be lost if this camp development project was to go ahead. (The Water Trails people who we spoke to were particularly alarmed because Gossip Island was to be a designated kayaker's camp... something that they had lobbied long for.) We even developed a Gossip Island website that soon began to receive thousands of hits.

Fortunately, there have been a few times in my life when opportunities and people came together at just the right moment to create an event with long-lasting impact. This was apparently one of them. Within six weeks of that evening in our Jones Island camp, the State Parks Commission reviewed our petition, together with testimony from dozens of other folks interested in Gossip Island. Some were local people, others came from as far as Spokane, hundreds of miles away in the eastern part of the State. To its credit, the Commission made the right decision to terminate the campground development project and to leave Gossip Island natural.

Delighted, Kanda and I quickly put together suggestions for a management plan that made Gossip Island a day-use only area with proposed annual monitoring to note any "human erosion" to the prairie system or sedum beds. I still visit the island nearly every summer and after many years of public use, there has been no noticeable habitat deterioration on the island. In fact, some of the casual trails that visitors have created help support at least two native plant species that do not compete well in the tall grass.

In the intervening years since the future of Gossip Island's little prairie and Sedum colony became more secure, several other of my favorite places have narrowly dodged the "bullet" of development. Just because a property may be held in the public domain does not mean that its flora and fauna are automatically protected. There are many reasons why the biodiversity of special places "fall through the cracks" and become diminished. For example, an inimicable administration can declare a property surplus and sell it outright, or the land can be swapped for a "better" parcel in some interagency land deal. Unfortunately, the mandate to protect biological values does not necessarily get transferred along with the deed of title. Consequently, I have become very alert to possible threats to public land and its special places.

In the concluding section of this book, "*Preserving Natural Areas in the San Juan Islands*," I discuss some of the dynamics of habitat protection and things that you and I can do to protect the natural heritage in our favorite places. From my own experience with Gossip Island, I have learned that we (the public) cannot protect a place that we know and love by keeping it hidden away and secret. Governmental policies often require that we "use it or lose it." The question is how do we go about doing this without disturbing or disrupting the sensitive life that makes these places so particular and worthy of preservation.

I hope that when you visit the special places described in this book you will respect the fauna and flora living there. This includes refraining from bringing your dog (even on a leash) and staying on established trails. I have witnessed many times the unwitting damage that energetic off-trail cross-country hikers can do. A misstep on a hidden bird nest or sensitive plant, such as a ground orchid, can completely destroy them.

"House-keeping" in natural areas can be an issue, too. Please pack out all of your trash, even your cigarette butts. Take nothing but memories. These are our natural areas, the last that we will ever have here in the San Juan Islands.

*Terry Domico*
*Friday Harbor,*
*San Juan Island*

# *ACKNOWLEDGMENTS*

A book is rarely the work of just one person and this book is no exception to that rule. I am greatly indebted to the patient labor of cartographer Eleana Pawl, whose maps not only illuminate these pages, but whose quiet enthusiasm has helped to shape and guide the entire project these past several years. There were also many other people who lent a helping hand in the creation of this book, some unknowingly. I would like to offer special thanks to a few, including my wife, Andrine, for your support of this project; to Denny Martel for the bush plane flight to make aerial photographs; to Henry Duvernoy for providing much-needed encouragement (and comic relief) via e-mail in my darkest hours; to Thor Hansen, former Lands Steward and Dennis Shafer, former Director of the San Juan County Land Bank, for ongoing discussions about protecting biodiversity on public lands; to Lincoln Bormann and Eliza Habegger, present Director and Land Steward, respectively, for continuing this discussion; to Jim Maya for the portrait sessions and your tolerance for my bigger mistakes; to Erik Schorr for accompanying me out to Saddlebag Island in the rain and for your "philosophical" enthusiasm for this project; to Richard Wright (the Wright stuff) for volunteering to create and maintain the "San Juan Islands Natural Areas Project" website; to Mark Goldsmith, "keeper" of the Priority Habitats and Species information for the WDFW for providing me with much-needed site-specific data over the years; to Jeff Vaughan for helping me to count and measure the Garry oak trees of Jones Island; to Kanda Kumar for your tireless dedication to habitat and bird conservation everywhere, especially in your home country of Malaysia; to Mickey Molnaire for much-valued help in providing me with a computerized book layout program and getting it to actually work; to Michael Kaill, for donating your valuable talent (and boat) to make our expeditions together most memorable; to Bill Engle and Keith Jones, the "core" of the San Juan Chapter of the Washington Native Plants Society, for your tips, advice, and volunteered help; to Bob Scott (retired Superintendent) and Peter Dederich (present Superintendent) of the San Juan National Historical Park, for offering your comments and for listening to my own; to my friends working with The Nature Conservancy, including Phil and Kathy Green (caretakers of Yellow Island), Peter Dunwiddie (ecologist), and Tony Scruton (caretaker of the Waldron Island preserves); to John Gamon, botanist with the Washington State Dept. of the Natural Resources's, Natural Heritage Program; to Dona Wuthnow, San Juan County Parks Superintendent; to Dave Castor and Chris Guidotti of Washington State Parks; to Dr. Eugene Kozloff (the "Koz") for your comments on the text of this book, and to my late friend, Steve Yates, who also knew and loved the San Juan Islands.

You have all enriched my life through your help and friendship ... and thus have made this book possible.

# HOW TO USE THIS BOOK

This book was designed to serve as a general field guide to selected natural areas in the San Juan Islands. International in its scope, the site-list includes locations in both the United States and Canada. Although most of the areas are found within San Juan County (Washington State), I have tried to include representative examples centered in the bioregion known as the Salish Sea.

There are sixty natural areas described in this book. The general location of these sites can be determined by using the "Natural Areas Locator Map" found on the following page. Each area has been assigned a number and is profiled in the text in chronological order as a separate chapter. Site chapters are further organized into related sections such as the natural areas found on Fidalgo Island or sites related to the Orcas Island district.

Each site description includes an overview map, a representative photograph and a short narrative essay depicting the premier qualities of the place. A key to the natural and man-made features depicted in each map can be found on page eight. Road directions and travel distances are usually calculated from the nearest ferry terminal. Species common names and scientific nomenclature are those which are currently in use. A special section entitled *"Preserving Natural Areas in the San Juan Islands"* has been included at the end of this book.

For newcomers to the region, it is a very good idea to supplement this book with detailed charts and topographic maps of the surrounding terrain.

*View westward from Mount Young, San Juan Island*

# Natural Areas Locator Map

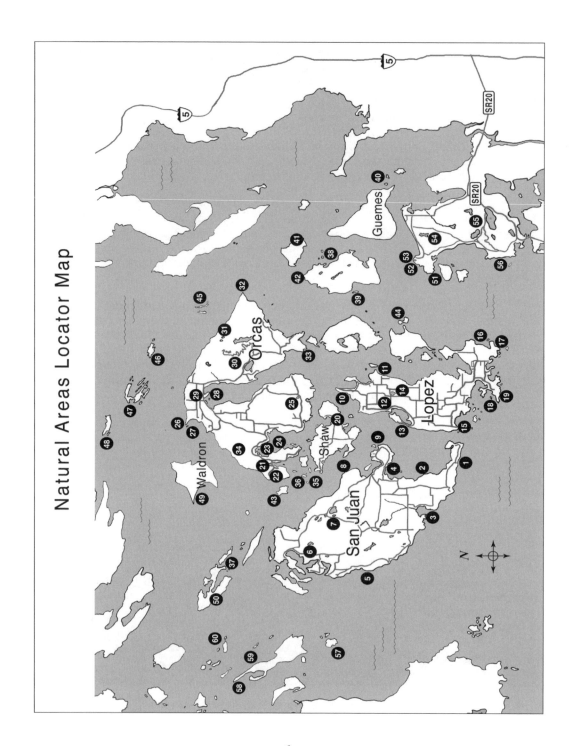

# Site Numbers

1. American Camp
2. Griffin Bay State Park
3. False Bay
4. Argyle Lagoon
5. Lime Kiln Area
6. English Camp
7. Sportsmans Lake Marsh
8. Point Caution
9. Turn Island
10. Big Tree Grove (Odlin Park)
11. Spencer Spit
12. Weeks Wetland
13. Fisherman Bay Salt Marsh
14. Hummel Lake
15. Shark Reef Park
16. Watmough Bay
17. Point Colville
18. Iceberg Island
19. Iceberg Point
20. Squaw Bay Headland

21. Cayou Lagoon
22. Frank Richardson Wildfowl Preserve
23. Skull Island
24. Victim Island
25. Killebrew Lake
26. Point Doughty
27. Freeman Island
28. Madrona Point
29. Crescent Beach Marsh
30. The Four Falls
31. Summit Lake
32. Lawrence Point
33. Obstruction Pass State Park
34. Turtleback Mountain Preserve
35. Yellow Island
36. Little McConnell Island
37. Gossip Island
38. The Cone Islands
39. Strawberry Island
40. Saddlebag Island

41. Mary Leach Natural Area
42. Cypress Island NAP
43. Jones Island
44. James Island
45. Clark Island
46. Matia Island
47. Sucia Island
48. Patos Island
49. Cowlitz Bay Preserve
50. Reid Harbor Marsh
51. Washington Park
52. Cannery Lake
53. Ship Harbor Marsh
54. Little Cranberry Lake
55. Mount Erie
56. Sharpe Park
57. D'Arcy Island
58. Sidney Island Spit & Lagoon
59. Mandarte Island
60. Rum Island (Isle-de-lis)

# KEY:

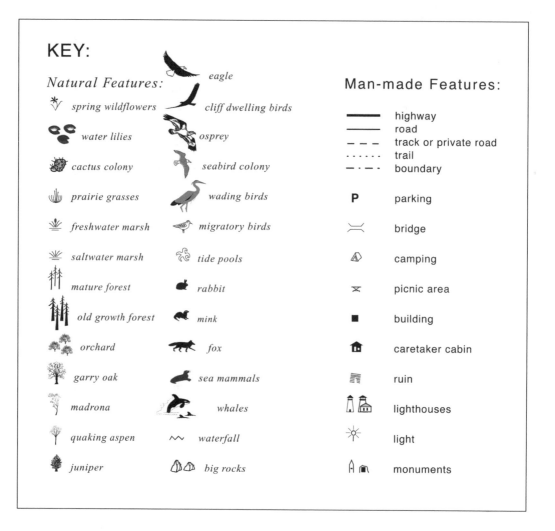

**Natural Features:**

eagle

🌱 spring wildflowers     cliff dwelling birds

water lilies     osprey

cactus colony     seabird colony

prairie grasses     wading birds

freshwater marsh     migratory birds

saltwater marsh     tide pools

mature forest     rabbit

old growth forest     mink

orchard     fox

garry oak     sea mammals

madrona     whales

quaking aspen     waterfall

juniper     big rocks

**Man-made Features:**

━━━ highway

─── road

– – – track or private road

· · · · · trail

– · – · boundary

**P** parking

bridge

camping

picnic area

■ building

caretaker cabin

ruin

lighthouses

light

monuments

8

# Part 1: THE REGION

## A. *Geography and Culture*

Between the mainland of northwestern Washington State and Vancouver Island, British Columbia, lies an island complex known as the San Juan Archipelago. Renowned for their scenic beauty and wildlife resources, this unique island group rests in an inland sea bordered by Vancouver Island and the Olympic Peninsula on the west and the mainland of Washington to the east. These waters, collectively known as the "Salish Sea," were vividly characterized by the late Steve Yates as "a long, brawny arm of the Pacific Ocean terminating in a handful of estuarine fingers gouged into the Puget/Fraser lowlands by sharp glacial fingernails." The Strait of Juan de Fuca is the gateway that connects this sea to the open ocean.

No one quite agrees on how many islands there are here in the Salish Sea. Some so-called "experts" say 786 at low tide, 457 at high tide, but they have missed the crucial distinction between an "island" and a "rock." In cartographer's terms, an "island" supports terrestrial vegetation (such as grass, trees and shrubs), a "rock" does not. By this definition, there are less than 250 "islands" in the archipelago.

Originally inhabited by Salish-speaking native peoples, the San Juan Islands were "discovered" by European explorers in 1791. The first to come were from Spain, who liberally bestowed Spanish names to the geographic features of the area. Then hot on their heels in 1792 came Captain George Vancouver, who claimed possession of the entire area for Great Britain. Of course, the British gave English names to their new discoveries and so renamed many of the Spanish titles. Today, our place-names are a mixture of the two languages.

In ensuing years, both Britons and Americans settled in the islands. The treaty of 1846, which established the boundary between the United States and what would eventually become Canada, left the location of the boundary through the San Juan Islands rather vague. Ownership was disputed and it was not until 1871 that arbitration finally awarded most of the San Juans to the United States.

Since then, the San Juans have been settled and developed along several lines including farming, limestone mining, fishing, and recreation. All of the major islands (except Cypress Island) now have roads, small towns or villages, and related developments. Today, recreational tourism is the region's most important industry.

# B. Geology

The basin in which the San Juan Islands are located is actually the northern part of a much larger physiographic depression, called the Puget Trough, that lies between the Cascade Mountains and the continental coast for the entire length of Washington State from Canada to Oregon. The Puget Trough is a glaciated feature in which the San Juan Islands are thought to represent just the tops of a submerged mountain range. These mountains may have once connected Vancouver Island to the mainland.

During the recent Pleistocene Ice Age ("recent" in geological terms), all of the islands were overridden by glaciers. In some areas the ice may have been more than a mile thick. The region's highest peak, 2,409 foot-high (735 meters) Mount Constitution on Orcas Island, bears glacial markings on its very top. The lowest point in the area, a 1,356 foot-deep (413 meters) trench in Haro Strait may have been carved out by these same glaciers as well. As the great ice mass pushed through the region, it apparently gouged out many of the other deep channels and bays scattered throughout the San Juan Islands.

Century by century, from perhaps 22,000 to about 17,000 years ago, this huge ice sheet surged and crunched southward over the top of what would eventually become the San Juan Islands. This was not the first giant ice sheet to affect the region. Evidence from seabottom corings suggests that at least sixteen other Ice Ages have occurred in this same region during the past two million years.

Sometime between 16,000 to 17,000 years ago, our most recent Ice Age reached its greatest limit of expansion. Then for the next 4,000 years, this great body of frozen water melted and retreated northward in uneven spurts, eventually exposing a completely altered landscape in its wake between 12,000 and 13,000 years ago.

The underlying bedrock of the San Juan Islands is composed chiefly of folded Paleozoic and Mesozoic sedimentary rocks. Almost everywhere, though, the Paleozoic layer has been intruded by a series of dikes and sills of basic igneous rock. This material is readily apparent in many places along eroded rocky coastlines where ridges often extend underwater, creating numerous reefs and shoals. Also visible across the landscape are the great piles of gravelly debris and till that the retreating glaciers dumped on top of this bedrock. In some places, bands of glacial till range from a few inches to hundreds of feet thick.

Soils in the San Juan Islands region are highly variable, with nearly one hundred types described. Not many of these soils are really good for farming, however. Typically, they are rocky and coarse-textured, extremely well drained, and poor in nutrients. However, a few soil types, such as those filling low-lying out-wash basins, are composed of extremely fine sand and clay. Most wetland areas in the San Juan Islands are underlain with these pulverous and highly compacted soils.

In the San Juan area's northern region, the basement rocks are generally sandstones, such as those found in the Sucia Island group. One striking feature of these rocks is their cross-bedding. Cross-bedding is created when a stream of water deposits sediment in layers that are inclined in the direction of current flow. When the direction of the current shifts, the angle of the bedding changes accordingly. Fossils found entombed in these layers suggest that, perhaps 50 million years ago, this once was a wide river plain covered in palmetto palms and other subtropical plants. The oldest fossils discovered in the San Juans appear to be more than 200 million years in age.

*Double-crested cormorants resting on a tidal rock*

## C. Climate and Weather

Most of the air masses reaching the San Juan Islands come from the Pacific Ocean. These maritime systems have a moderating influence on the climate, creating two basic seasonal divisions over the year. From late autumn, through winter and into spring, prevailing westerlies and southwesterlies produce a wet season that peaks in November and December. These counter-clockwise systems often push one wet and windy storm event after another into the region. Snowfall is rarely heavy and the growing season will occasionally persist along the shoreline throughout the entire year.

*Douglas fir trees sculpted by prevailing winds (San Juan Island)*

Beginning in May and peaking in August, northwesterly and northeasterly winds begin to prevail, usually resulting in an intermittent dry season. For the most part, these clockwise breezes are driven by a large, somewhat stable, high-pressure system that often appears over the eastern north Pacific during summer months. A large rain event in late September, however, often signals the "end of summer."

The San Juan Islands lie in the so-called "rain-shadow" of the Olympic Mountains and Vancouver Island and therefore generally receive less total rain than most other parts of western Washington. The region's average annual rainfall usually varies between 21 to 29 inches (53.3 to 73.5 centimeters) per year making this one of the driest coastal areas in the Pacific Northwest. Rainfall totals can also differ markedly from island to island during any given year.

The mean high temperature for the San Juans is about $70^0$ F. ($21^0$ C.). The highest recorded temperature was around 100 degrees F. ($37.7^0$ C.) and the lowest fell to just below - $8^0$ F. (- $13.5^0$ C.). Midday temperatures between $75^0$ to $80^0$ F. ($24^0$ to $27^0$ C.) during summer months are not uncommon.

The average water temperatures in the seas surrounding the San Juan Islands are rather cold, ranging from a nippy $44^0$ F. ($6.6^0$ C.) in February to a still chilly $51^0$ F. ($10.55^0$ C.) or so in August. However, some of the "back" bays that receive little tidal flushing can warm up enough in midsummer to allow comfortable swimming. Access to most of these sites requires local knowledge.

During periods of spring tides there can be a 13-foot (4-meter) tidal difference within a six hour duration. Such a large variation in water heights requires nearly constant movement of a huge volume of water, creating strong and dangerous currents throughout the region. This is especially true in the narrow passes between some of the islands.

## D. *Important Biological Features*

Cool sea temperatures, strong currents caused by large tidal differences, and expansive estuaries fed by glacially-spawned mainland rivers such as the Skagit and the Nooksack have combined to create a unique marine region of amazing wealth and biodiversity. Giant kelp forests harbor rock fish, ling cod, starfish, sea cucumbers, wolf eels, sea urchins, sponges, and giant octopus. During the brief periods of slack water between tidal exchanges, scuba divers can explore spectacular underwater rock walls covered with giant sea anemones and colorful shrimp. Eelgrass (a species of seagrass) forms broad meadows on the bottom of numerous shallow bays, which in turn become the nurseries for many of the fish and shellfish species found within the region.

At the top of this assorted list of diversity are the orcas (killer whales) that are attracted to the Salish Sea to feed on its rich pulses of migrating salmon and numerous harbor seals. Other marine mammals that are fairly common in the region are harbor porpoises (now considered endangered worldwide), northern elephant seals, Steller sea lions (in early spring), Dall's porpoise, and the occasional California gray whale or humpback whale.

13

Then there are the islands themselves. The ecology of small and isolated land-masses has long fascinated me and is the reason why I originally came to live in the San Juans. Relative to the mainland, an island's smaller size necessarily restricts the number and extent of possible habitats. This leads to the development of a unique floral and faunal community on virtually every island.

Island communities are the hotbed for evolution of new species (and ideas). Since the region's islands were exposed to the air by receding glaciers some 12,000 or 13,000 years ago, there has been continuous colonization by plants and animals new to the area. Some have flourished, while others unable to compete or find a supportive niche have vanished. The process continues to this day, with new arrivals often aided by human transportation. Two of the newest species to show up on our beaches within the past decade or so, the purple varnish clam (*Nuttallia obscurata*) and a shore plant, European searocket (*Cakile maritima*), seem to be here to stay.

Due to their isolation relative to the mainland, some long established species are becoming uniquely endemic. A study of the rare brittle cactus (*Opuntia fragilis*) in western Washington has revealed the apparent biogeographic development of at least four different island "morphs" of this plant. On some islands the spines are larger and differently colored from the average individual; on other islands the pads have a new shape and color.

When viewed from the sea, most islands (especially the larger ones) appear to be covered with the mixed evergreen/deciduous forest typical of western Washington. There are differences here, though. Some tree species such as Pacific madrona (*Arbutus menziesii*) and shore pine (*Pinus contorta*) are generally much more common here than on the mainland. This is especially true along the well-drained slopes above the seacoast.

Stands of large virgin timber, some over 300 years old, still exist in isolated pockets among the islands. Here can be found exceptionally large specimens of Douglas fir, western red cedar, Sitka spruce and bigleaf maple. A few of these groves have received governmental protection by being included into State or County park lands. Others are being privately protected.

In exposed situations, usually on the south side of islands, we often find open areas that contrast sharply with the nearby forest. These well-drained sites are subject to drying winds and receive the maximum amount of solar energy during the day. Consequently, they have very low soil moisture conditions during the summer. This harsh environment attenuates the growth of most trees and woody shrubs.

Instead, these locations often support grassland prairies that are nowadays usually dominated by several varieties of introduced "orchard grasses." Occasionally (especially near the seashore), native species such as Idaho fescue (*Festuca idahoensis* var. *roemeri*) will still prevail. Lichen-covered rock outcroppings are common in these areas. Spring wildflowers such as Hooker's onion, harvest brodiaea, camas, chocolate lily, few-flowered shootingstar, and sea blush can also be found in these settings, especially where there has been little grazing or disturbance.

At the other end of the soil moisture extreme are the islands' wetlands. Most of them are found in depressions underlain by impervious bedrock, saturated clay-like soils, or deep organic muck. They range from limited emergent wet meadows to fresh water marshes and open water lakes. At the heads of some shallow bays and lagoons, where fresh water streams and the sea are able to interact, small estuaries and salt marshes of incredible productivity have been created.

Open sea, varied shore-forms, rocky outcrops, prairie grasslands, deep forest, hidden springs, sparkling lakes, exposed mud flats and jutting cliff-faces. These are some of the habitats that shape the natural areas of the San Juan Islands.

*The rare brittle cactus (Opuntia fragilis) sports a bright yellow flower in June.*

# E. Some Information for Visitors

The city of Anacortes, located approximately halfway between Seattle and Vancouver, B.C., is considered to be the gateway to the San Juan Islands for people coming from the American mainland. This community is located on Fidalgo Island at the western terminus of State Highway #20, about sixteen miles west of Interstate 5. Road access to the island is via bridges across Swinomish Slough and Deception Pass.

From Anacortes, a state-operated ferry system serves four of the largest and most inhabited islands in the San Juan group: San Juan Island, Orcas Island, Shaw Island and Lopez Island. In addition, there is international ferry service to and from Sidney, B.C. on Vancouver Island.

Often by-passed by visitors perhaps because one can easily drive there, Fidalgo Island is actually one of the more interesting islands in the San Juan Islands group. Because the City of Anacortes has inherited a unique legacy of wildland that surrounds much of the community, Fidalgo Island supports a number of outstanding natural areas. (Six of these sites are profiled in Part 7.) I can only hope that the city's future government and natural resource managers will have the good sense to protect these areas from logging or development interests.

Thirty-two of the natural areas profiled in this book (more than half) are accessible via automobile transport (followed by hiking along trails). Another twenty-eight of these sites, however, can only be reached by boat. Exploration by sea-kayak is an intimate way of exploring the island coastlines and has become very popular throughout this region in the past decade or so. Kayaks now outnumber conventional vessel traffic: the sailboats and cruisers that traditionally spend the summer months "fossicking" the back bays of the San Juan Islands. There are a growing number of rental and guided kayak tour companies in and around the islands.

Most of the natural areas described in this book are strictly day-use only. However, twenty of these sites (mostly in State and County parks) have camping facilities associated with them. Please camp only in designated campsites as camping outside of these areas will ultimately impact and degrade the nearby habitat. Pack out all of your trash.

Also, please do not bring your dog for a walk or romp in one of these natural areas. (I cannot stress this too strongly.) Dogs frighten and chase ground-nesting birds, deer, otter, raccoons and other wildlife. Trail bikes and motorcycles are a similar nuisance. Besides tearing up sensitive trails and plants, motorbikes also terrify wildlife with their incredibly loud noise. Leave your bike at home and try walking for a change. You won't regret it.

# Part 2: SAN JUAN ISLAND

Covering an area of just over 55 square miles, San Juan Island is the second largest landform in San Juan County. It is also the location of the county seat and most developed urban center, the town of Friday Harbor. Presently, more than 7,000 people (nearly half of the county's population) live on San Juan Island.

San Juan Island is served daily by Washington State Ferries and chartered air services. A full range of visitor accommodations and tourist activities are available here, including kayak expeditions and whale-watching tours.

Of the 9 natural areas described in this section, two of them (Griffin Bay State Park and Turn Island) can only be accessed by private boat or kayak. These two locations are also the only two places listed in this section where overnight camping is allowed. For information about camping fees and local campsite restrictions, call the office of Lime Kiln State Park at (360) 378-2044 or self-register on-site.

# 1. American Camp (San Juan Island National Historical Park)

**Size and Ownership:** 1228.6 acres  (Federal Land managed by the National Park Service.)

**Facilities:** Trails, picnic tables, drinking water and toilets at visitor center.
[No camping, dogs must be kept on a leash.]

**Access:** From the ferry in Friday Harbor, drive up Spring Street and turn left onto Mullis Street.  Continue south along this winding road (out of town it becomes known as Cattle Point Road) for about 7 miles until you see national park "welcome" signs. *By boat:* There are no facilities for larger boats, but kayaks and dinghies can be beached along South Beach during periods of calm seas.

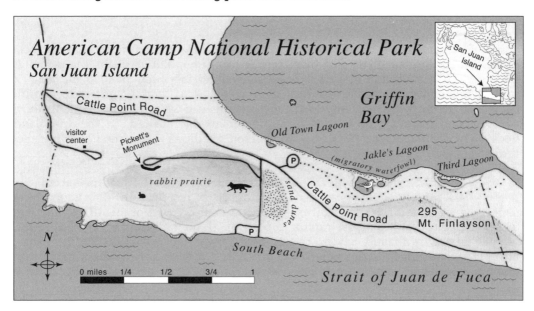

**American Camp** was designated to become part of the San Juan Island National Historical Park by Congress in 1966.  Although the park's primary function is to commemorate the infamous "Pig War" boundary dispute between the Americans and British (1859 to 1872), it is well known for its stunning marine vistas. (The park receives nearly a half million visitors each year.)  American Camp also contains several exquisite natural area ecosystems which are much less frequented.

**Rabbit Prairie** is roughly delineated by Cattle Point Road and the road to South Beach.  This broad grassland covers more than a third of the park's total area. Besides providing a grand sweeping vista, this prairie also exhibits evidence of a formerly large population of "San Juan Rabbits."  Here and there you can occasionally

19

still see the odd rabbit crouching by an entrance hole leading down to their communal warrens. These bunnies are actually European rabbits (*Oryctolagus cuniculis*) which were introduced to the islands on several occasions during the late 19th and early 20th centuries.

Regardless of their origin, these animals have "naturalized" in the islands and, until recently, were the most important ecological factor affecting this prairie. They change the area's vegetational composition by plant browsing and soil disturbance through their digging. The park's present administrators seem to be committed to restoring this prairie to something resembling its early European settlement condition and are making a determined effort to eliminate rabbits within the region. However, wholesale removal of these animals will have far-reaching effects not only to the prairie's plant community but to the predators which depend on them for food. Already we are witnessing a dramatic drop in the numbers of raptor birds seen in the area.

Rabbits may not be as serious a problem as some ecologists and park officials think. During the late 1970s, San Juan Island's rabbit population came to a peak. At that time it was estimated that there were somewhere between 250,000 and 400,000 rabbits inhabiting the island. Under their tremendous grazing pressure, prairie grasses were cropped short and, more importantly, successional woody plants (such as shrubs and trees) were kept from becoming established on the grassland. Because of decreased competition from grasses, wildflowers bloomed in abundance creating brilliant springtime displays.

The rabbits were prey for people and predators alike during this period. (For many years rabbit hunting was a popular sport on the island.) Predatory birds especially benefited from the rabbit's presence and for most of the 1970s, San Juan Island supported the densest raptor population (bald and golden eagles, rough-legged hawks, red-tailed hawks, great-horned owls and goshawks) in the United States. But then came the big population crash, and rabbits all but disappeared from much of the island.

What happened? There were many theories to explain why the rabbit population changed so dramatically and this was a common topic of discussion at the local taverns. Suggestions from former rabbit hunters and naturalists ranged from overpredation by introduced ferrets, to toxins created by overgrazed plants, to lethal poisons set out by parks staff. The real reason was revealed to me in 1990, a half a world away.

In 1987 and 1988, I became intrigued by the question of why the rabbit population wasn't rebounding as quickly as expected... after all, it had been nearly ten years since the crash. So I decided to study rabbit predation on a ten acre site, using my parked car as an observation blind. For nearly six months I drove to American Camp twice a day - in early morning and evening - to watch the behavior of the rabbits and to record incidents of predation. What I discovered surprised me. There were the usual raptors (eagles and hawks and the like) but the leading predators at that time were feral cats (replaced by red foxes several years later).

There were three resident female cats living on my study site and a male who showed up now and again. Between the four of them, I estimated that they were each killing and eating a cub (a young rabbit) a day. I'll never forget a comment made by my mother when she accompanied me on one of my evening trips. "Why, it's just like a miniature Serengetti," she exclaimed after having watched a cat go down into a burrow and emerge with a small rabbit kicking in its jaws. Not more than ten feet away, two adult rabbits watched warily as the cat devoured the cub.

During Christmas of 1990, I was in Canberra, Australia, attending an office party for the CSIRO (an organization similar to our USDA). I was on a research assignment to study kangaroos at the time and had just returned from a very hot three-month-long stint in the outback. Standing around with a blessedly cold beer in my hand, people came over, one by one, to meet the "Yank." The usual conversation would start with, "Where ya from, mate?" and I would answer with, "San Juan Island." "Yeah? And where's that?" was the usual response...until one gentleman said, "I know San Juan Island... you've got a rabbit problem. At least you did until I took care of it." My jaw (and my beer) dropped to the floor.

He was a microbiologist and worked with a rabbit plague virus. Sometime around 1976, he received a request from "certain parties" on San Juan Island to send over a couple of vials of the virus to help control their rabbit problem. "It worked real well, didn't it?" he asked me.

"The disease only affects rabbits but does not kill every individual animal... and after fifteen years or so its effects become negligible as the population recovers and grows immune to that particular strain of virus," he told me. The cat and raptor predation that I had been studying was simply slowing the rabbit population's recovery and was not the reason for the crash.

More importantly, in the areas on the island where the rabbit populations had been eliminated or severely reduced, the decreased grazing pressure has allowed weedy introduced grasses to gain the upper hand and crowd out many of the wildflowers, reducing the prairie meadow biodiversity. Also, because the tree seedlings were not being nipped in the bud, a successional forest of young Douglas firs has crept across large sections of former grassland. Without help from the rabbits, it will take a lot of determined human effort to return these areas to prairie conditions. Introduced species such as the European rabbit are not *always* a bad thing for sustaining biodiversity.

There are also some interesting birds to be seen on the Rabbit Prairie. In late summer and autumn, nervous flocks of black and yellow American goldfinches

(Washington's state bird) can be seen foraging for nutritious seeds among the fluffy tops of Canadian thistles. Another bird that I look forward to seeing each year are the meadowlarks perched on old fence posts, warbling out their distinctive call.

Of special interest to serious bird watchers, American Camp and the surrounding vicinity supports the only documented nesting population of the Eurasian skylark (*Alauda arvensis*) in the United States. Introduced from Europe to Victoria, British Columbia, back in 1903, some of these birds eventually found their way to American Camp where they took up residence. By 1973, their population had grown to nearly 20 pairs.

Although they look a bit like a large sparrow with drab brown-streaked plumage, skylarks can be distinguished by their white-marked wing-tips, breast, and outer tail feathers. They also hold their wings in a distinctive "half open" position when resting. While this bird is not a particularly colorful species its melodious and complicated trilling call, which is performed while hovering a hundred or so feet above the ground, is an absolute delight to hear.

The current lark population size is unknown but certainly has been reduced by the increased presence of foxes. Skylarks inhabit open grassy areas and build their nests on the ground, putting them at risk to predation. There is some evidence that these birds may actually be seeking safer nesting areas. Recently, I have observed them on both Long Island and southern Lopez Island, where foxes and feral cats are not such a serious threat. There have also been reported skylark sightings on Whidbey Island and the Olympic Peninsula.

The **Sand Dunes** cover an area of about 20 acres located in the "wedge" of land formed by Cattle Point Road and the road leading down to South Beach. This is an active system that is slowly becoming stabilized by the encroachment of rhizomatous grasses. Geologically speaking, large sections of the entire prairie contained active sand dunes at one time or another but this remnant is all that presently remains.

Sand dunes create a specialized habitat for native pioneer plants such as the yellow sand verbena (*Abronia latifolia*) which thrives here, forming the largest colony of this species in the San Juan Islands. It survives the summer drought by storing food and moisture in a huge fleshy taproot that can weigh up to 20 pounds. Hidden in the sand throughout the long winter, these roots send a dozen or so prostrate stems radiating out from its crown during the growing season.

Its thick leaves are sticky and the thousands of sand grains that adhere to each one probably help hold the stems in place during periods of strong wind. A coating of gritty sand also makes these succulent leaves less palatable to browsing animals. In June and July, hundreds of "heavily" sweet-scented bright yellow sand verbena flower clusters can be seen dotting the dunes.

*Center of the dunes (looking south)*

Other pioneer plants that can be seen on the dunes include Canadian thistle, beach lupine, small-flowered blue-eyed Mary, red sorrel, shepherd's purse, miners lettuce, pink-flowered cranesbill, small-flowered fiddleneck (*Amsinckia menziesii*) [so named because its stalk of tiny yellow flowers resembles the head of a fiddle], dune grass, and beach morning-glory (*Convolvulus soldanella*).

Although several grass species, bracken, and a few other plants are slowly encroaching on the bare sand and thus are tending to stabilize these dunes, I've noticed that the active portions of the dune system can quickly enlarge during an exceptionally strong storm. Visit this site during a strong wind and you will see "flights" of sand streaming past your legs. Here and there, the eroding wind exposes a few knarled yellow sand-verbena tap roots. They look like miniature tree trunks from some ancient and long-forgotten forest. Bit by bit, the dunes are moving inland across the island's southern isthmus.

Once the grasses take hold and stabilize the system, however, all dune movement essentially stops. Unable to withstand competition from the smothering grass, sand verbenas and other specialized wildflowers soon disappear. In this particular location, however, it is the introduced wild rabbit that assists in the maintenance of a healthy dune system. Their constant nibbling helps keep the grasses down and their burrows dug into the stabilized dunes create scour spots where the wind can erode away the sand. Rabbits are so important in helping to keep this dune system "alive" that it likely would have disappeared many years ago without them.

The **Three Lagoons** are located about a half mile apart on the Griffin Bay side of the isthmus leading out to Cape San Juan. (All three lagoons are linked by trails maintained by the Park Service or you can walk along the beach at mid-to-low tides.)

The first one, *Old Town Lagoon*, sits on part of the site formerly occupied by the island's first village, San Juan Town, which accidentally burned down on July 4, 1890. It can easily be seen by driving out Cattle Point Road and turning off into the parking area at the Jakle's Lagoon trailhead. The lagoon can be seen just above the beach a couple of hundred yards downhill.

This lagoon appears to have been naturally formed and was probably a "void" area in the settlement of San Juan Town. Whatever its origins, it is presently an active salt marsh system. Smaller and more exposed than the other two lagoons, it often dries completely during the summer. During the drying process, as the water becomes shallower and shallower, this small spot attracts large numbers of shorebirds, including yellowlegs, snipe, and sandpipers. Several species of ducks and red-winged blackbirds are also commonly seen here. The berm of sand and gravel separating this lagoon from Griffin Bay seems to be stable and is not regularly breached by winter storms. To the northwest, just up the beach from Old Town Lagoon is a muddy flat, about an acre in extent, that is covered by driftwood. This is a prehistorical lagoon site that is now rarely flooded because accumulating soils have built it up beyond the influence of high tides.

*Jakle's Lagoon* is situated further along the coast of Griffin Bay below the north side of 295-foot-high Mount Finlayson. (Created by glacial outwash, Mount Finlayson is essentially a large gravel berm.) Considered to be the "crown jewel" of San Juan Island's lagoons, Jakle's Lagoon is a semi-isolated body of saline water separated from Griffin Bay by a gravel bar covered with beachgrass and driftwood. Water level in the lagoon is usually well above mean water in Griffin Bay and is, at present, exchanged with the sea only through one exit during storms or during periods of extreme high tides.

Except for these times of flood, water flow is generally out of the lagoon and into Griffin Bay. During extreme low tide, the water level in the lagoon can drop about 1/16 of an inch an hour. The lagoon itself has been the subject of several detailed studies by students from the University of Washington. With an average depth of 7 feet (maximum 13 feet), this ±12 acre body of water is essentially held in two lobes. The smaller lobe, with a maximum depth of 6 feet, becomes separated from the main lagoon during summer as the water level drops. (Both portions of the lagoon experience heavy algal blooms during this season.) In winter, as water heights increase, both lobes join together once again to form a single lagoon. Sill height for the lagoon system is about 6.6 feet above mean high tide.

*Driftwood logs clutter the surface of Jakle's Lagoon*

Truly a separate ecosystem (an isolated salt lagoon with tidal influence) much of the research has been focused on the copepods (*Acartia species*) [small planktonic crustaceans] that feed on the algae and in turn are fed upon by the millions of larval sticklebacks that inhabit the lagoon. [Three-spined stickleback (*Gasterosteus aculeatus*) is the lagoon's dominate fish species but several other species including yellow shiner perch, Pacific herring, and various sculpins can also be found there.] The fish enter and leave the lagoon only during the periodic flood tides that temporarily connect it to the rest of the sea. During these brief times I have witnessed tens of thousands of young fish urgently migrating through the narrow channel into Griffin Bay.

The landward side the lagoon is surrounded by mature forest. (The area was logged in the late 1890s - early 1900s, back at a time when they used the springboard system for felling old-growth. The notches that supported these springboards can still be seen in some of the old stumps.) In spring there are many nice calypso orchids on the forest floor surrounding the lagoon. The edge of the forest is also a favored hangout for belted kingfishers.

Further east along the gravel beach sits **Third Lagoon**, a shallow depression with an openwater salt marsh system separated from Griffin Bay by a pebbly accretion shoreform. Surrounding this open water are good examples of the region's typical salt marsh plants such as pickleweed (*Salicornia virginica*), salt-tolerant grasses like *Distichlis spicata*, sea plantain, and salt lambsquarter. The high water mark surrounding the lagoon is littered with heaps of driftwood which are home to a myriad of voles and the occasional river otter or mink.

In the San Juan Islands, tidal lagoons are rare landforms that require special environmental conditions in order to exist. Eroded sediments from nearby cliffs must be carried and deposited by longshore currents during storm events, creating a sandy or gravelly berm that separates an enclosed body of water from the rest of the sea.

Third Lagoon is roughly 420 feet long and 80 feet at its widest point and perched slightly above the open bay. A temporary narrow channel through the berm allows for the interchange of water at extreme high tides. Just beyond the driftwood strand on the inland side of the lagoon is dense mature second growth forest. In summer the lagoon tends to dry up a bit and attract shorebirds. In winter it's filled with water and attracts many ducks and other waterfowl. Bald eagles are often seen perching on the trees above the lagoon.

## 2. Griffin Bay State Park

**Size and Ownership:** 14.76 acres  (State Land managed by Washington State Parks.)

**Facilities:** Trail, picnic tables, camping and pit toilets. [No water.]

**Access:** *By boat:* There several mooring buoys for larger boats just offshore but kayaks and dinghies can be beached on the gravelly shore during mid-to-high tides.

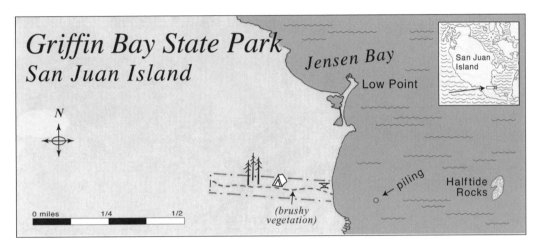

This rather hard-to-find little park can only be publicly accessed by water. It is a long narrow property with just 343 feet of mid-to-low bank waterfront that can easily be missed when looking for it from a boat offshore. The best visual clue is a lone wooden piling festooned with purple martin birdhouses located almost due west of Halftide Rocks. From just north of the piling, a "welcome" sign announcing the park can be seen on shore. There is also a shore-mounted reflector strip for locating the park at night with a spotlight. (The GPS coordinates for the entrance to the park are 48° 28' 59" N, 123° 00' 55" W.)

Above the 5-to-6-foot high waterfront bank is a mowed grassy area that serves as a picnic area. A grassy track leads inland through this narrow strip of land (approximately 300 feet wide by 2,000 feet long) where campsites can be found just inside the forest at the upper end.

Ranging from sea level to 85 feet in elevation, this property displays a prime example of shrub/scrub and young forest succession. Formerly a cleared sheep pasture, this area has been destocked and left fallow for more than thirty years. The previous grassland is now being overtaken by woody shrubs such as Nootka rose and snowberry, which are in turn being replaced by black hawthorns and then by young firs and pines. (This patchy successional transition can easily be viewed as you walk along the mowed track leading up the middle of the property.) The upper end of the park is dominated by a semi-mature second growth Douglas fir forest.

Birdwatching in this area can be quite good. Commonly seen species include cedar waxwing, goldfinch, American robin, rufous-sided towhee, MacGillivary's warbler, chestnut-backed chickadee, pileated woodpecker, bushtit, white-crowned sparrow, vesper sparrow, and various other "little brown jobs" that are usually found in this kind of environment. Great-horned and barred owls can sometimes be seen roosting in the tall trees at the upper end of the park.

*Successional growth bordering the inland track*

# 3. False Bay

**Size and Ownership:** 200+ acres of intertidal sand flats (State owned tidelands, managed as a Biological Preserve by the University of Washington.)

**Facilities:** Parking turnout, no toilets. [No fires, camping, or clamming.]

**Access:** To reach False Bay from Friday Harbor, head west out of town on Spring Street, then turn left at the intersection with Douglas Road. Continue along this road (becomes Bailer Hill Road) until the left turn onto False Bay Road. False Bay is about a mile from this turnoff.

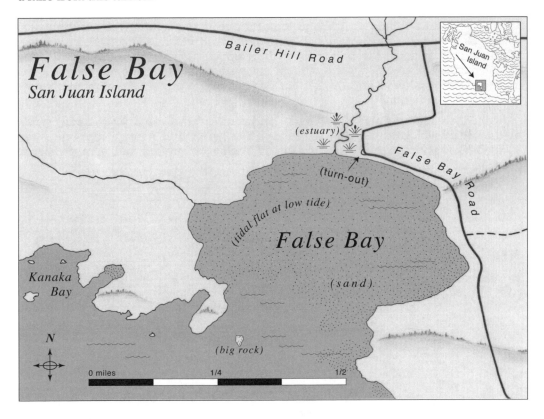

**False Bay** is a large, roughly circular, shallow, sand-bottomed inlet. At high tide, the bay looks ordinary enough; a broad sheet of semi-sheltered water with its south-facing entrance connected to the deep waters of Haro Strait. But after the turn of the tide, a broad wave-rippled sandflat soon appears. At low tide, the entire bay is nearly drained and during periods of extreme low tide, it is possible to walk with rubber boots out into the bay for more than half a mile. Be careful, though... when the tide begins to come in again, water levels can rise quickly. More than once I have watched a party of would-be explorers fleeing in an undignified manner for shore.

The bay is managed as a biological study area for the University of Washington. Indeed, there is a rich assemblage of marine life to discover under exposed rocks and in the shallow pools left behind by the receding tide. Many of these creatures such as the shore-crabs, shrimps, mud-dwelling amphipods, sand worms, barnacles, bent-nosed clams, and tidepool sculpins are small and easily overlooked. But there are larger animals here, too. Glaucous-winged gulls, north-west crows, Heermann's gulls, great blue herons, and even bald eagles can be regularly seen on the sandbars in search of temporarily stranded fish and other nutritious morsels.

One unusual little creature to look for out on the sandflats is a bubble snail called "Diomedes aglajid" (*Melanochlamys diomedea*) which feeds on the brown haze of micro-detritus lining the bottom of shallow pools. It is a rounded mollusk, about 2/3 of inch long, whose shell is almost covered by its overlapping mantle. The gelatinous material in its egg masses has been shown to protect developing embryos from solar UV radiation.

At the head of False Bay, a small driftwood-choked estuary has been created by the stream which drains San Juan Valley. This lovely little estuary supports ducks, sticklebacks, sculpins, baby chum salmon, Pacific cinquefoil, and a rare patch of graceful arrow grass (*Triglochin concinnum*).

*False Bay at low tide*

## 4. Argyle Lagoon

**Size and Ownership:** ± 12 acres (University of Washington, managed as a Biological Preserve.) Public land that is municipally owned and managed by the Port of Friday Harbor surrounds the lagoon on three sides. [Except for a 1.69 acre reserve, most of the north side is privately owned.]

**Facilities:** Parking turnout, boat ramp, toilets, no water. [No fires, camping, or clamming.]

**Access:** The lagoon is only about a mile out of town. From the ferry landing in Friday Harbor, head straight up Spring Street and turn left on Argyle Avenue, take another left on Pear Point Road and then right at Jackson Beach Drive. As you come down the hill, you'll see the lagoon below on the right. There is parking near the public toilets.

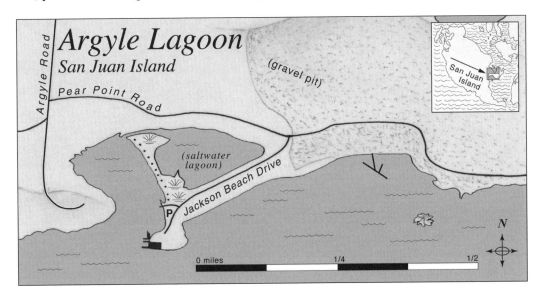

Argyle Lagoon
San Juan Island

Argyle Road

Pear Point Road

(gravel pit)

San Juan Island

(saltwater lagoon)

Jackson Beach Drive

P

0 miles   1/4   1/2

N

**Argyle Lagoon** is enclosed by a sand/gravel spit that may have been formed by the outwash of glacial meltwater during the end of the last ice age. Indeed, most of the high ground surrounding the lagoon is composed of glacially deposited sand and gravel. An 1897 US Army topographical map indicates the presence of a high "feeder" bluff located just northeast of the lagoon. (Most of this bluff has since been mined, separated into various grades of sand and gravel, and hauled away.)

Although it is connected to the sea by a shallow tidal creek at its northern end, the lagoon's water level is remarkably stable and often only varies between 4 to 8 inches between extreme high and low tides.

Most of the lagoon and its enclosing salt marsh is off-limits to the public. (A long stretch of its shoreline is fenced along Jackson Beach Drive. Jackson Beach itself is a popular municipal park.) There is, however, limited public access for viewing the lagoon along a trail that begins near the toilet block and runs north along the top of the gravel berm on the west side of the lagoon.

*Argyle Lagoon and surrounding salt marsh*

Surrounded by a salt marsh dominated by pickleweed (*Salicornia virginica*) and saltgrass (*Distichlis spicata*), this lagoon is an excellent place for birdwatching. Stalking through the shallows, great blue herons spear small fish, while shorebirds such as sandpipers and dunlin probe the mysteries of the nearshore mud. Ducks and other waterfowl can frequently be seen foraging in small groups on the water. This is often a good place to view several sea-duck species, such as scoters, that are usually found offshore in more open water.

Because the salt marsh and shore of the lagoon are very sensitive habitats (especially to trampling footsteps), take care not to leave the trail or to unleash pet dogs and allow them to run free.

# 5. Lime Kiln Area

**Size and Ownership:** 247 acres of public lands (39.6 acres State Land managed by Washington State Parks, 207.4 acres San Juan County Land Bank.)

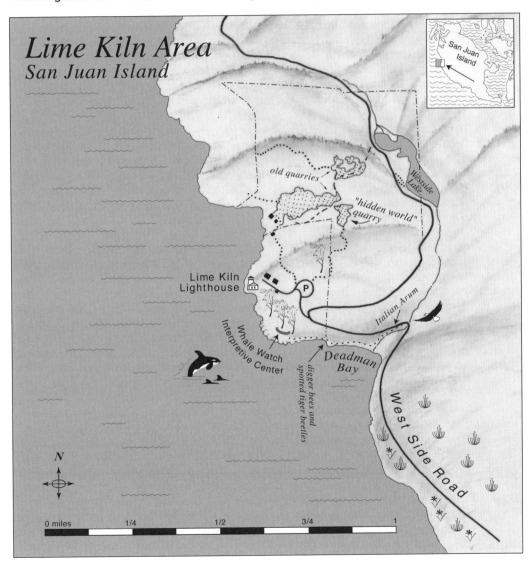

**Facilities:** Parking turnouts (County), parking area (State), whale-watch interpretive area (State), toilets (State), drinking water (State), picnic tables (State), trails. [No fires or camping, dogs must be kept on leashes.]

**Access:** To get to the Lime Kiln Area from Friday Harbor, head west out of town on Spring Street, continuing left at the top of the street near the big water tank. Here the road name changes to San Juan Valley Road. Continue out of town, turning left at Douglas Road (1.7 miles from ferry). Travel south on Douglas Road, which then becomes Bailer Hill Road when the road turns sharply right towards the west (3.4 miles from ferry). Continue along this route (road becomes West Side Road along the way) until the Lime Kiln State Park welcome sign is seen at the junction of a sharp right turn. *By boat:* There are no facilities for boats, but kayaks and dinghies can be beached along Deadman Bay during periods of calm seas.

The **Lime Kiln Area** is a conglomeration of public lands that include some of the most dramatic coastal views in Washington State. In addition to its outstanding scenic values, an amazing number of priority habitats are also found here. The name "Lime Kiln" comes from a limestone quarry and wood-fired lime-rendering kiln industry that operated here from the late 1800s until about 1939. The quarry was finally closed to all commercial use, including being a source of crushed rock, in the early 1980s. It is now part of the San Juan County Land Bank.

Using the lighthouse at Lime Kiln State Park as our landmark reference, a short trail leads south to the "whalewatch overview." This viewpoint, complete with interpretive signs, is the most frequently visited spot in the area. Nicknamed "Whale-watch Park," it is one of the best places in the world to see orcas (killer whales) from shore. Occasionally one will surface not more than fifty feet from a thrilled audience standing on the rocks. During the summer months, especially in August and September, Pacific salmon tend to congregate along this shore during their breeding migration back to their natal freshwater rivers and streams. (Salmon are a favored food of many of the orcas in the region.) Minke whales, harbor porpoise, Dall's porpoise, and harbor seals are also frequently seen from this shore.

In the area surrounding the lighthouse, you may notice a deciduous tree with smooth reddish-orange bark and shiny dark-green leaves. Here and there the bark can be seen peeling away from the trunk in paper-thin sheets revealing a greenish layer beneath. This is Pacific madrona (*Arbutus menziesii),* a member of the heath family. (Spanish settlers apparently called it *"madroño"* [masculine] and through the English this eventually became *"madrone,"* and now *"madrona"* [feminine], which in Spanish is not remotely connected to any tree. Incidentally, most Canadians in the region simply call it *"arbutus."*) Madrona trees don't tend to occur in pure stands and this is one of the few places in the State of Washington where they occur in such densities. The most impressive grove (being the purest and largest) is about 60 yards southeast of the lighthouse, about halfway along the trail to the whalewatch overlook. (Incidentally, the masses of red berries that are produced in the fall are edible.  They taste a bit like applesauce when boiled and then mashed.  Although most of the berries are born too high for easy picking, they are an important autumn and early winter food for several species of migrating birds.)

Continue hiking east along the coast past the whalewatch overlook and you will soon come to **Deadman Bay**.  (It's said to be the crime site of the first white man to be murdered on the island.)  Today the area is managed for day-use only by the San Juan County Land Bank and is known as Deadman Bay Preserve.  Above the bay is a boulder-lined turnout that allows a car or two to park off the road.  From here a trail leads down to the bay itself.

This area contains a number of unique biological features.  For example, flowing into the head of the bay is a seasonally intermittent stream that has created a fine little wetland complete with clumps of the large-leafed western skunk-cabbage (*Lysichiton americanum*) whose incandescent yellow spathes brighten many of the region's swamps and bogs in early spring.  Unless there has been a period of heavy rain, the water in the creek usually subsides into the gravel of the upper beach and then disappears.  However, under the sea (down around the low tide zone) the fresh water percolates to the surface again.  This special phenomenon supports a little shrimp-like organism, an amphipod that's only found in a few widely scattered spots in the world.  It has no common name that I know of and is known to scientists only as *Paramoera bucki.*

*Deadman Bay*

35

The San Juan Islands are the result of a mixture of complex geological processes involving igneous, sedimentary and metamorphic materials. At Deadman Bay, the creek that flows into the head of the bay traces a fault-line that is, in fact, the dividing line between two geological formations. All of the underlying rock on the property west of the creek is igneous in origin and has been designated by geologists as Deadman Bay Volcanics. This geological unit is dominated by red and green pillow basalt, breccia, and tuff interbedded with pods of nearly pure limestone. Trace element chemistry indicates that the formation was probably erupted in an off-shore setting and was moved to its present location through the actions of oceanic plate movement. In contrast, all of the rock that creates the southern slopes of Mount Dallas and the Westside Scenic Corridor are metamorphic in origin and are composed entirely of gray and green ribbon chert and Garrison schist.

On the west end of Deadman Bay beach stands a small sand/clay bluff created from the sediments of glacial outwash. If you carefully examine this 10-foot-high structure in the spring (May-June) you might notice small downcurved tubes made of mud jutting out of the embankment. These are the entrances to the nests of digger bees (Anthophora occidentalis). Sometimes the face of the embankment is completely riddled with their small holes, each protected by a little clay chimney. Most active in late spring and early summer, the bee's favorite food seems to be the yellow monkey-flower (Mimulus guttatus) from which it drinks nectar with its extremely long tongue. Because of this blossom's very long corolla (floral tube), digger bees may be the monkey flower's primary pollinator. Digger bees are not common on San Juan Island and are only found in a few locations. It may be "just" coincidence, but these are also the same areas where yellow monkey flowers seem most plentiful.

This clay bank also serves as a hunting habitat for another locally uncommon insect species, the green-tinted tiger beetle (Cicindela tranquebarica). These jewel-like hyperactive beetles may be seen hunting small insects and spiders around the base of the embankment and out on the rocks. Occasionally, I have witnessed some amazing struggles between these beetles and would-be prey twice their size. Usually the tiger beetle wins, but sometimes things go badly and the predator itself gets eaten.

**Lime Kiln Preserve** can be accessed by trail about ¼ mile north of Lime Kiln Lighthouse. As mentioned earlier, it includes an area of historic limestone mining and processing and is managed by the San Juan County Land Bank. The remains of the two wood-fired lime kilns can be seen perched on the hillside above the sea. A hike up the trail into the old quarry itself is well worth the effort. The quarry is actually composed of one main pit and twelve smaller "satellite" pits carved out of solid rock. The most important geological feature on this property is the presence of a large deposit of limestone (the Cowell Deposit), which consists of three major irregular lenticular bodies of limestone interbedded in basalt. Much of the limestone is light gray in color and finely crystalline in texture. (There are samples scattered everywhere.) Some pockets of this limestone are said to contain fossilized specimens of the fusulinid *Neoschwagerina* that are thought to be somewhere around 200 million years old.

While you are exploring this area it is well to bear in mind that this was a former industrial site. For decades, people blasted the rock with dynamite and gouged out the broken rubble with bulldozers. At length, it was finally abandoned to the process of reclamation through natural processes. Because the surrounding tree community had been left relatively intact and the disturbed areas allow to revegetate, these same man-made features have now become highly productive and diverse wildlife areas. In low spots, small wetlands have formed, attracting numerous frogs including the threatened red-legged frog (*Rana aurora*). One quarry wetland even supports a small grove of black cottonwood (*Populus balsamifera* var. *trichocarpa*), a tree species that is rather rare in the San Juan Islands. Some of the little caves created by the piles of huge boulders shelter bats and other small mammals.

On the relatively undisturbed lime-rich soils surrounding the quarries are three species (two plants and a mollusk) that are rarely seen in such abundance anywhere else in the region. Spring (late April through mid-May) is the best time to encounter them on the moss-covered forest floor. The first one is an extremely odd plant, a little-studied vegetative form of *Triteleia* (*Brodiaea*), a member of the lily family. Instead of flower-ing, like a normal Brodiaea, this one forms small bulbs and has the appearance of being a three to four-inch-tall onion. However, it has no onion-like smell about it at all. Also found in these same moss-beds are the handsome lined land-snail (*Monadenia fidelis*) and col-onies of the lovely calypso orchid (*Calypso bulbosa*) a ground orchid also known as the "fairy-slipper."

*Calypso orchid*

**Westside Lake** lies about one-half mile northeast of the lighthouse, as the crow flies. It is most easily accessed by continuing north for a half-mile or so on West Side Road, past the entrance to Lime Kiln State Park. This 0.4 mile-long lake lies in the trough formed by the juncture of the two geologic units mentioned earlier. Its eastern shores are fronted by a steep slope that eventually leads to the top of 1,062-foot-high Mount Dallas.

The lake was created sometime during the latter half of the Twentieth century by logging, dredging and then damming a natural wetland. Records are scanty, but it appears to have been created by a real estate development scheme which ultimately failed. It now serves as an important wildlife corridor and is a good example of what I have come to term as a "man-made natural area."

Averaging only about 6 to 7 feet deep (14 feet in its deepest spot) the lake can be accessed from several road turnouts provided along its length. Although it does not afford good fishing, it does attract a lot of waterfowl, especially during winter. This is the best place that I know of to see the attractive ringnecked duck. Bufflehead, baldpate, and wood ducks are also common. Because most of the lake is hidden from direct view from the road, some areas in the lake become "crowded" with ducks during the migratory season. (No hunting allowed.)

The forest surrounding the lake is a mixed transitional woodland consisting of Pacific madrona, a few large Douglas firs, some young firs, red alder, the occasional western red cedar, and a lot of broad-leaf maples. Remnants of the original wetland with its deep organic soils and colonies of western skunk-cabbage can be seen in the wooded swale just beyond the northern end of the lake.

## 6. English Camp (San Juan Island National Historical Park)

**Size and Ownership:** 529 acres (Federal Land managed by the National Park Service.)

**Facilities:** Trails, picnic tables, and toilets near parking lot. [No camping or fires, no drinking water, no bicycles on trails, dogs must be kept on leashes.]

**Access:** From the ferry dock in Friday Harbor, drive up Spring Street and turn right onto Second Street. Continue west through the first stop sign intersection, turning right at the second stop sign. Heading out of town, follow Roche Harbor Road until it is joined by West Valley Road (about 7.8 miles from Friday Harbor). Turn left onto West Valley Road and continue for about 1.3 miles until you see the signs directing you into the park. *By boat:* There is a substantial dinghy dock about two-hundred yards northwest of the white blockhouse. Good anchorage for larger boats can be found further out in Garrison Bay. The combined entrance to Garrison Bay and Westcott Bay can be accessed from the eastern side of Mosquito Pass, which leads between Henry Island and the northwest end of San Juan Island.

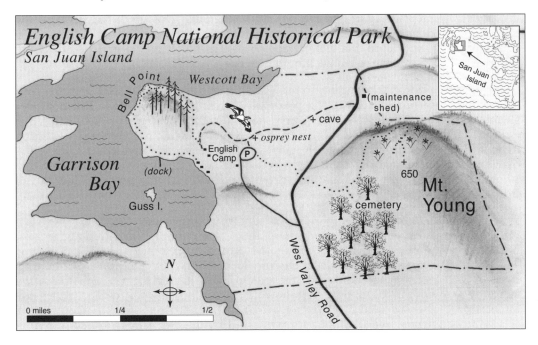

English Camp National Historical Park
San Juan Island

English Camp is part of the San Juan Island National Historical Park designated by Congress in 1966. Although the park's primary function is to commemorate the infamous "Pig War" boundary dispute between the Americans and British (1859 to 1872), this section also contains several exquisite natural areas. Incidentally, visitors to the Barracks building (one of the original structures from the British occupation) may notice a very large big-leaf maple (*Acer macrophylum*) growing nearby. Until a strong windstorm removed nearly half of its crown in the 1980s, this nearly 300 year old tree was considered to be the largest specimen of its kind in the world. The remaining portion is still quite impressive.

Mount Young Trail goes from the top of the parking lot through a tall stand of Douglas fir mixed with Pacific madrona (the smooth orange-barked tree), red alder, and red cedar. After approximately 250 yards of gentle uphill grade, the trail crosses the pavement of West Valley Road and proceeds through a section of dark woods nearly devoid of undergrowth. In spring, however, this is a good area to look for two species of unusual ground plants, pine-drops (*Pterospora andromedea*) and spotted coralroot (*Corallorhiza maculata*). You will find them growing in the deep shade beneath the trees lining the trail. Both of these species lack chlorophyll and subsist with the help of an associated symbiotic fungus.

Rounding a bend, the trail becomes more open. Here, vines of the unusual Oregon manroot (*Marah oregonus*), also called wild cucumber, can be seen twining over shrubs and tree branches. Unlike our garden variety of cucumbers, however, the prickly fruits of these plants are deadly poisonous. The seeds are so toxic that they were used as a means of committing suicide by some northwest Indians. Also growing along the trail in this vicinity are numerous honeysuckle vines that when in bloom are very attractive to rufous hummingbirds.

A short side track leading to the British cemetery branches off from the main trail. This small cemetery, with its poignant inscriptions of the dead left behind is surrounded by a large grove of Garry oaks (*Quercus garryana*) [also known as Oregon white-oak]. My earliest memories of San Juan Island include these venerable trees with their deeply fissured bark, which can be up to four inches thick. This grove is one of my favorite spots... every tree is so dramatically individual. In the summer when they are in full leaf, the ground is spattered with pools of deep shade from the dark green canopy.

As wildlife habitat, Garry oaks are almost unsurpassed. Those hollows up in the limbs attract cavity-nesting birds; small reptiles and amphibians hide under loose bark; then there is the "mast crop" when the acorns drop to the ground and support various wild birds and mammals, including turkeys and the ubiquitous Columbian black-tailed deer. When decayed, the oak's fallen leaves form a rich mulm that supports a number of showy wildflowers including purple camas (*Camassia quamash*), blue-eyed Mary (*Collinsia parviflora*), and Henderson's shooting-star (*Dodecatheon hendersonii*). The habitats created by the oak groves are so important that biologists have labeled it a "keystone" species. More than sixty-eight species of plants and animals (including some endangered ones) are associated with Garry oaks. Many of these species would have a difficult time surviving if the oaks were to suddenly disappear.

Until recently, very few of the oaks in the San Juans were reproducing. A survey conducted during the 1970s revealed that none of the Garry oak trees on San Juan Island were less than 36 years old. Also, many of the oak groves in the region have become beset with a great number of small Douglas fir seedlings growing under the canopy of many of the trees. As these young firs grow, they increasingly compete with the oaks for light and moisture. If this process continues without natural or man-made intervention, the oaks eventually lose and die out.

*Garry oaks at the foot of Mount Young*

Both of these problems may be ultimately related to the wildfire suppression policies of our modern society. Fire is a natural agent in the evolution and maintenance of many species of native plants including the oak groves. Thirty years ago, for example, this particular grove used to support an amazing spring wildflower show. But the grove was neglected, even after it became part of the national park. Over the intervening years, forest succession and invasive grasses wiped out most of the flowers. Many of the oak trees also suffered and began to die. Eventually the problem became so apparent that the park service was forced to intervene. In July of 2003, after an absence of nearly fifty years, fire was reintroduced to this grove. I was on hand to witness the historic event, which involved more than forty firefighters and their various trucks and equipment. The "wildfire," which was kept under strict

41

control, was allowed to burn the understory growth that was threatening the oaks. Although this burning will have to be done periodically in the future in order to maintain the grove, the wildflowers now have a chance to stage a "come back."

**Mount Young** is accesssed by returning to the main trail and continuing your climb to the summit. Along the way the trail passes through a zone of deep forest and ocean spray bushes (*Holodiscus discolor*) that create a tunnel-like canopy above the path. Some of the moss-covered boulders beside the path support colonies of broad-leaved stonecrop (*Sedum spathulifolium*) and licorice fern (*Polypodium glycyrrhiza),* named for its licorice-flavored rootstocks. Open areas along the way often reveal glimpses of wild turkeys, turkey vultures, bald eagles, sea crows, rufoussided towhees and black-tailed deer.

The view seaward from the top of Mount Young (650 feet) has spectacular vistas of nearby Henry Island, Vancouver Island and the Canadian Gulf Islands. Across Haro Strait can be seen the jagged skyline of Victoria perched on the southern end of Vancouver Island.

*Henderson's shooting-star*

If you look carefully at the exposed rock on the summit of Mount Young, especially where the thin mantle of soil has been worn away by rain, you can see excellent examples of glacial striations (marks left by an advancing glacier). They are particularly nice towards the backside of the summit, near the grassy areas. At this point, the Vashon Lobe of the last great ice-age glacier surged directly towards the spot where the city of Victoria would eventually be built.

**Bell Point Trail** begins near the dinghy dock in Garrison Bay at the northwest corner of the parade ground surrounding the old blockhouse and other historic buildings. It is a pleasantly scenic loop trail that winds along the shoreline above a high embankment through patches of tall forest containing a few fire-scarred old-growth trees that were mature even before the first European set foot on the island. There are some nice stands of Pacific madrona on the hill slope, backed by taller Douglas fir and a few western hemlocks. Here and there is an occasional granite boulder (erratic) left behind by receding glaciers.

The rather sparse shrub layer, dominated in places by wild rose, salal, ocean spray, and snowberry has created an excellent habitat for the island's only squirrel species, the northern flying squirrel (*Glaucomys sabrinus*). You are not likely to see one of these lovely creatures as they are very shy and completely nocturnal in their habits. I have observed them, however, flitting from tree to tree on quiet moonlit nights. Interestingly, one of their favorite foods are the small underground "mushrooms" that develop from the mycorrhizal fungi that grows under the surface of the forest floor and which links every tree together with their threadlike mycelium. These fungi are symbiotic with the trees and help them to absorb vital nutrients from the soil. The fungal spores which pass unharmed through the squirrel's digestive system are spread through the squirrel's droppings, thus helping to ensure the health of the forest.

At **Bell Point** a little spur trail leads off to the very tip of the point. All along the shore near here are shell middens, evidence of long use of this area by native peoples for gathering clams and as a camping area.

In May and early June, near where the main trail reaches its most northerly apex before turning towards the south, look for calypso orchids (*Calypso bulbosa*) growing out of the leaf litter and moss. Here and there are also a few white broad-leaved starflowers (*Trientalis borealis* ssp. *latifolia*). Also called Indian potato, I've eaten their small little tubers... not bad when cooked but hardly worth the bother unless you are starving.

Bell Point Trail encircles the small "hillock" (105 feet altitude) that comprises most of the point. Along its east side, the trail passes through dog-hair thickets and some forested wetlands. Across a meadow to the southeast you can see an osprey nest on the bare top of a large old-growth Douglas fir which stands like a beacon.

Along the car track that leads north from the base of the "osprey tree," the diligent investigator will find a small overgrown trail that leads to one of San Juan Island's geological anomalies: a limestone cave. Located at the head of an old quarry, this small cavern leads back for a distance of about 75 feet to where the passage has filled in with mud. There are natural "windows" in the roof which illuminate much of the passageway, so it never gets totally dark during daytime in most of the cave. (Incidentally, this cave was used in a dramatic scene from Laszlo Pal's production, *"Journey to Spirit Island,"* filmed in the San Juan Islands during the early 1980s.)

# 7. Sportsmans Lake Marsh

**Size and Ownership:** Sportsmans Lake is approximately 87 acres with a mixture of public and private ownership.

**Public Access Points and Facilities:** Boat launching beach (State), [No toilets, drinking water, fires or camping.]

**Access:** From the ferry dock in Friday Harbor, drive up Spring Street and turn right onto Second Street. Continue west through the first stop sign intersection, turning right at the second stop sign. Heading out of town, follow Roche Harbor Road until you see the lake and the public access sign on the left.

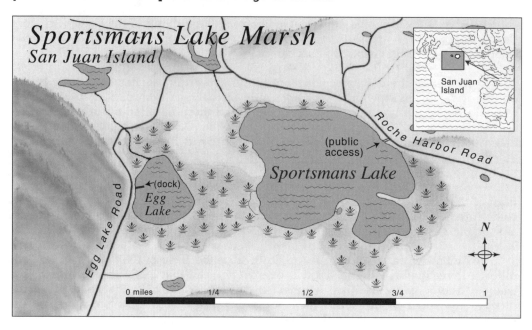

The lake and marsh can only be explored by small boat (canoes and kayaks do best here). Since almost all of the lake is bordered by private lands, do not trespass by "beaching" your boat and tromping around without first obtaining permission (preferably in writing) from the land holder. Actually, it is a good idea to avoid walking around in the wetland margins as they are both very difficult to traverse and extremely sensitive to damage from human footsteps.

Access to the lake is via a small sliver of public land that extends from Roche Harbor Road down to a small beach at the water's edge. An informal parking strip for vehicles can be found alongside the main road.

**Sportsmans Lake Marsh** invites slow and careful exploration. It is replete with cattails, yellow pond lilies, and other water-loving plants. During the spring and summer seasons, Virginia rails, soras, red-winged blackbirds, and marsh wrens twitter, croak, and cluck from within clumps of reeds while swallows of several species chase aerial insects above open water and repeatedly perform seemingly daring "touch and goes" on the lake's surface. In many places the marsh is bordered by thickets of willows and Pacific crabapple which are complete with their own signature birds such as willow flycatchers, yellow warblers and the occasional cedar waxwing. Osprey are a common sight around the lake. (The lake has been stocked with largemouth bass and bluegills [pumpkinseed sunfish].)

*Sportsmans Lake Marsh*

In the dead of winter, at the end of December and through the first weeks of January, the lake and marsh periodically host their most spectacular visitor, the trumpeter swan (*Cygnus buccinator*). Enduring freezing sleet and snow, I have watched flocks of up to twenty of these elegantly huge birds while they foraged and explored the margins of the marsh. Interestingly, when the weather really turns cold the birds often confine themselves to the middle of the lake. (Shallow water is the first to freeze when a lake freezes over, so the swans may be avoiding potential entrapment and exposure to any predators who might venture out onto the ice in anticipation of an easy meal.)

## 8. Point Caution Preserve

**Size and Ownership:** More than 483 acres with nearly 3 miles [15,630 feet] of shoreline. (University of Washington.)

**Facilities:** None. [No toilets, drinking water, dogs, fires or camping.]

**Access:** From the ferry dock in Friday Harbor, drive up Spring Street and turn right onto Second Street. Continue west through the first stop sign intersection, turning right at the second stop sign. Heading out of town, follow the road to the right (University Road) when it "Y"s at the edge of town. Park in the parking lot at the Reception Center.

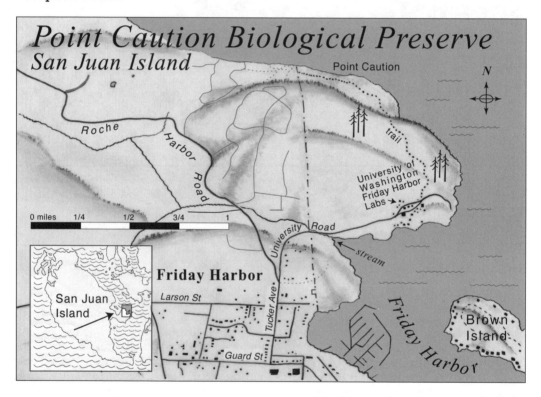

The land comprising **Point Caution Biological Preserve** (this includes the University of Washington Friday Harbor Marine Labs complex) was originally set aside during the late 1800s as a military reserve. This was one of six military reserves created in the San Juan Islands as part of a plan to protect the three entrances to Griffin Bay (where ships from the U.S. Navy "Great White Fleet" could be safely hidden from enemy eyes). The scheme was abandoned, however, shortly before

46

World War I with the advent of aircraft. After declaring the land "surplus," Congress transferred "ownership in trust" to the University of Washington for purposes of establishing a "marine station."

As you enter the complex of buildings comprising the U. of W. Friday Harbor Labs, you will see a sign asking visitors to check in at the office. After gaining permission to walk the Point Caution Trail, stroll on up the paved road past the cookhouse and housing area to where a fire protection trail with a cable strung across its entrance leads off to the left. A sign at the entrance reads: "No mountain bikes, no wheels, no smoking in wooded areas, no dogs allowed, picking of wildflowers prohibited." (This is a Preserve, so please obey these requests.)

The trail is about 1.5 miles in length and offers no return loop. A slow walker can complete a round trip in about an hour and a half. Quite a few locals, students, and lab staff use this trail for exercise in the morning, so be prepared to meet a jogger head on now and then. (Most of them, however, are finished and back to work by 9:30 AM.) Near its far end, the track begins to peter out, eventually terminating on a gravel road that serves a residential area west of the preserve.

*Tall timber at Point Caution Biological Preserve*

Photographs made in the early 20th Century show that the area containing the preserve was much more exposed at that time, as large parts of it had been cleared to create pasturage for gazing sheep. After the University took possession, the forest was allowed to reclaim these open areas and now little evidence of its agricultural history remains beyond the odd scrap of rusted fencing wire.

The first part of trail passes through a mixed transitional forest containing some very tall examples of Douglas fir, grand fir, and western hemlock. Broad-leaf maples and red alders are also present. Some of the largest specimens of Douglas fir (remnant individuals of old-growth known as '"wolf trees") have blackened fire scars going up their trunks as high as 40 feet. It is obvious that wildfire was part of this forest's ecology sometime in the past.

As the trail penetrates deeper into the forest, you will come to an area of wind-toppled trees lying crissed-crossed like jackstraws. (Most likely these are victims of our famous 1990 wind storm which blew over thousands of trees around the San Juan Islands.) Notice the shallow "pancake" of roots that were ripped up when the tree fell. Many of the coniferous trees in our region are very shallow-rooted, which seems to be an adaptation to growing in thin rocky soils

About 1/2 mile up the trail, just behind the crest of a low divide there is a sudden transition from an open forest dominated by Douglas fir and hemlock to a more closed forest dominated in places by western red cedar and a much denser shrub layer. (Some of the cedars are quite large; several measured more than 5.5 feet diameter [dbh]). This occurs at the highest point on the trail (164 feet altitude) and in some places the cedars are so densely profuse that they appear to create a nearly solid green wall.

The two main reasons for this remarkable transformation appear to be "more water and less sun." From this point onward the land slopes in a northerly direction and because north-facing slopes receive less sun (being typically shaded during summer afternoons and for most of the late-autumn, winter, and early spring), rain and surface ground water do not evaporate as fast as on south-facing slopes. The wetter ground favors cedar and denser underbrush. Usually the transition in forest types, however, is not quite so abrupt as it is here.

Some of the wildlife that I have observed along this trail include mink, river otter, raccoon, rose-breasted nuthatch, brown creeper, varied thrush, Swainsons thrush, fox sparrow, red-crowned kinglet, western fly-catcher, northern flicker, hairy woodpecker, and pileated woodpecker. Northern flying squirrels have been reportedly sighted here. In mid-spring watch for ground-loving orchids growing alongside the trail.

## 9. Turn Island

**Size and Ownership:** 33.5 acres (Federal Land managed by Washington State Parks.)

**Facilities:** Mooring buoys, picnic tables, camp sites, and pit toilets. [No drinking water.]

**Access:** *By boat:* Turn Island is located 1.6 nautical miles east of Friday Harbor, just off the eastern side of San Juan Island. There are several buoys for mooring larger boats and beaches for landing kayaks and dinghies. Turn Island can also be easily reached by paddleboats launched from the little park located just off the sharp turn in Turn Point Road on San Juan Island.

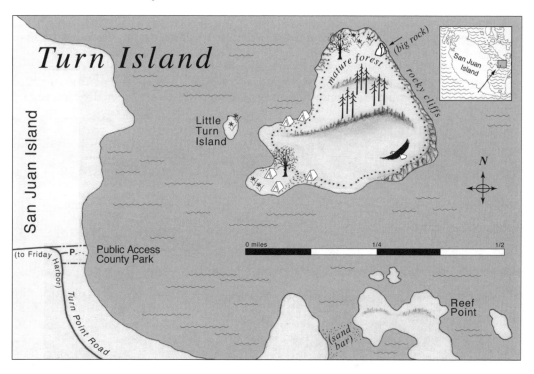

    **Turn Island** is one of my favorite stopovers whenever I'm boating in San Juan Channel. The entire island is designated as a US Fish and Wildlife Sanctuary, with camping and picnicking allowed on its southwest end. I like to spend a few days here every year.

With a just over a mile of coast to explore, there is a 0.85 mile-long loop trail that follows the shoreline around the island. The highest spot is in the center of the island at 104 feet but there are no trails leading to it. (The island's interior remains relatively untouched and contains some limited but excellent examples of Douglas fir dominated old-growth forest on well-drained rocky soils.) It also contains an active bald eagle nest and some superb specimens of Pacific madrona (*Arbutus menziesii*).

Along the trail on the northwest end of the island is a small stand of Garry oaks wedged in between a grass-covered rocky bald and the coniferous forest. These are the survivors from a time extending back for hundreds of years when there were many more oaks on the island. Without the intervention of human management, however, even this remnant will eventually disappear. (In spring [late April through early May] there is a very nice display of wildflowers on the rocky balds surrounding these oaks and out on the very northern end of the island.)

As you follow the path around the island you will eventually encounter a huge granite boulder (more than 8 feet high) that blocks the trail and forces a detour around it. This is a fine specimen of a glacial erratic. Thousands of years ago, during the last big ice-age, this stone was carried away from its bed-rock source in British Columbia by an advancing glacier and dropped here when the ice finally melted.

*Large granite boulder deposited by receding glacier*

# Part 3: LOPEZ and SHAW ISLANDS

Lopez and Shaw islands are the least developed of the ferry-served San Juan Islands. Lopez Island (named after Gonzales Lopez de Haro in 1791), the third largest island in San Juan County, is about 11 miles long and 4.5 miles wide. Its total area coverage is a little over 29 square miles. Although there are no "towns" per se on Lopez, there are some visitor accommodations available. Lopez Village, located at the north end of Fisherman Bay, is the largest retail center on the island.

Shaw Island, named after naval officer John Shaw during the 1841 Wilkes Expedition, is the smallest of all the ferry-served islands. Covering an area of 7.7 square miles, it has a resident population of only about 250 people. Except for a dozen campsites offered at Shaw Island County Park, there are practically no visitor amenities on the island.

Of the 11 natural areas featured in this section, two sites on Lopez Island (Big Tree Grove and Spencer Spit) and the Shaw Island site (Shaw Bay Headland) offer nearby campsites in the parks associated with each natural area. Contact the offices of San Juan County Parks at (360) 378-8420 or Spencer Spit State Park at (360) 468-2251 for updated information on camping fees and campsite availability.

## 10. Big Tree Grove

**Size and Ownership:** 85.25 acres [Odlin County Park.] (San Juan County.)

**Facilities:** Trails, picnic tables, public boat dock, boat launching ramp, campsites, drinking water and toilets.

**Access:** From the ferry terminal on Lopez Island, go south on Ferry Road for about one mile and turn right at the Odlin County Park sign. *By Boat:* Odlin County Park is located in a small bight on the northeast side of Upright Channel about one nautical mile south of Upright Head. There is a small public dock and float that can handle most deeper-draft vessels and a broad sandy beach for landing kayaks and dinghies.

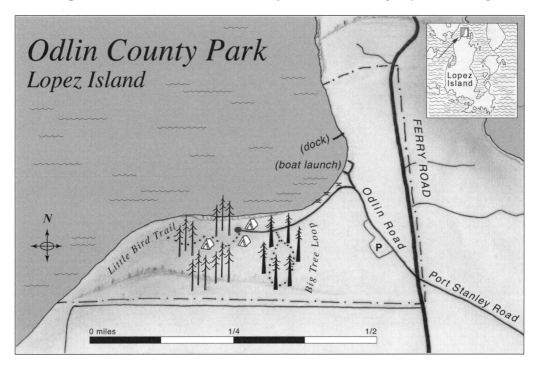

In two separate acts of Congress (on April 17, 1926 and January 21, 1929), San Juan County was "awarded" (for payment of $1.25 per acre) several abandoned military reserves for "recreational and public-park purposes." Facing Upright Channel on the northwest side of Lopez Island, **Odlin County Park** was one of those old reserves. Incredibly, this popular beach-front park also contains one of the most impressive groves of relic old-growth conifer trees remaining in the San Juan Islands. Just why these trees were not cut down and turned into firewood and lumber sometime during the last two centuries remains unclear.

The forest surrounding the grove appears to consist primarily of typical mixed transitional mature second-growth forest composed of white fir, western red cedar, western hemlock, Douglas fir and red alder. Within the grove, however, stand twenty-seven exceptionally large specimens of Douglas fir (*Psuedotsuga menziesii*). Some of these magnificent old trees are more than 6 feet in diameter and one-hundred feet tall. All of them are veterans of wildfire and exhibit charred fire-marks as high as 20 to 30 feet up their trunks.

The **Big Tree Loop Trail** is easy to find. Just after the beach frontage campsite road enters the forest you will see a toilet outbuilding. Following along both

*A cluster of old-growth Douglas firs*

sides of a small brush-filled creek gully, the trail begins and ends just behind this outbuilding. The far end of the trail crosses the creek via a plank bridge and loops back to the campground.

As you wander through this avenue of big trees, notice that their bark appears exceptionally thick and that most of their limbs begin very high up on the trunk. Both of these features are adaptations that serve to protect the tree from damage by wildfire. The thick bark acts as heat insulation, protecting the tender tissues lying beneath it and high limbs protect the vital canopy from the reach of all but the very largest forest fires.

Interspersed within the grove are numerous younger trees, which line both sides of the gully. The understory here typically consists of ocean spray, salal, sword fern, bracken fern, salmonberry, trailing blackberry, stinging nettle and wild rose. In late summer look for the intricate webs of the harmless dome-building spider. This is also a good location to see two birds that seem to prefer the forest: the winter wren and the rufous-sided towhee.

After visiting the big tree grove, you might want to stay a while longer and take a nice walk up the beach to Upright Channel Park, about a mile and a half to the west. A steep clay embankment fronts the sand beach for much of the way.

Galerina *mushrooms growing on the forest floor*

# 11. Spencer Spit

**Size and Ownership:** 128+ acres [Spencer Spit State Park.] (Washingon State Parks.)

**Facilities:** Trails, picnic tables, campsites, drinking water and toilets. [Dogs must be kept on a leash.]

**Access:** From the ferry terminal on Lopez Island, travel south on Ferry Road for about one mile and turn left onto Port Stanley Road and left again after 2.5 miles onto Baker View Road. After 0.5 miles Baker View Road turns sharply to the right. The entrance road to Spencer Spit State Park is on that corner. *By Boat:* Spencer Spit is located on the northeast side of Lopez Island just west of Frost Island. There is good anchorage both north and south of the spit and the gravel/sand beaches are suitable for landing kayaks and dinghies.

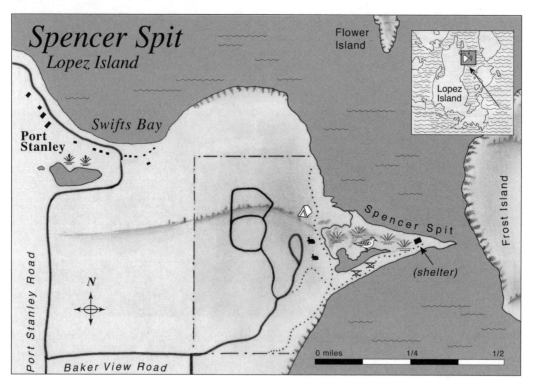

About 24 acres in size, **Spencer Spit** comprises less than one-fifth of the total area encompassed by Spencer Spit State Park. (Except for a disjunct colony of thicket-forming Sitka alder [*Alnus viridus*], most of the park is vegetated by the typical mixed transitional coniferous forest that often occurs on the well-drained upland soils of the San Juans.) The spit, however, holds the largest and most significant accretion shoreform salt marsh in the region.

Spencer Spit (named after an early settler) was created by the combined action of waves and longshore currents that conveyed and deposited sand and gravel eroded from the steep shoreline bluffs located nearby to the north and south. This is an ongoing process, as transported material from these "feeder" bluffs is continually precipitated onto the beaches of the spit by this method. The spit's almost symmetrical triangular shape is due to sand being deposited in nearly equal amounts on both its north and south beaches.

The extreme tip of the spit, however, migrates seasonally with changes in the direction of prevailing winds; winter storms force the tip to the north and in summer, winds from the north causes it to curve slightly south. Strong tidal currents in the narrow channel between the spit and Frost Island constantly erode the growing tip, preventing it from reaching across and connecting to the opposite island. Even so, the spit extends more than a third of a mile out from its base on Lopez Island.

The "crown jewel" of Spencer Spit is the shallow lagoon and salt marsh that has become established in its center. One theory maintains that the lagoon was formed when two developing prehistoric sand-spits joined into one, trapping a low spot between them. However it was created, the lagoon now actively fills and drains during large tidal exchanges through a connecting stream to the neighboring sea. (The shape of this stream slowly changes over time and now appears quite different from the maps created during early European settlement.)

The first several inches of material on the bottom of the lagoon and its joining stream consists mostly of dark sticky mud. This mud is not lifeless; it contains a myriad of worms, snails, larval fish, small crabs and other crustaceans. In fact, these small saltwater marsh estuarine systems are extremely productive... much more than an equal-sized area of forest or sea. Unlike the forest, where energy gets stored in the form of wood for many decades or even hundreds of years, the energy in an estuarine system tends to be utilized almost immediately. It's continually assimilated and doesn't have a chance to build up dead wood, so to speak.

Spencer Spit's salt marsh and lagoon is the critical habitat and home to many kinds of unique plants, birds and other animals. It's not uncommon to see mink, river otter, raccoon and numerous species of ducks and shorebirds here. In fact, the lagoon appears to be an important stopover for migrating waterfowl. I've witnessed mixed aggregations numbering into the upper hundreds during both the spring and autumn migrations. One such flock included pintail ducks, both greater and lesser yellowlegs, godwits, blue-winged teal, mallards, golden-eyes, bufflehead, American mergansers, sanderling, dunlin, numerous gulls, a western grebe, and two great blue herons. Other types of birds that visit this area seasonally include the least sandpiper, belted kingfisher, Canada goose, black oystercatcher, golden turnstone,

Bonapart's gull, pigeon guillemot, red-winged blackbird, osprey, sharp-shinned hawk, and the occasional bald eagle.

For wildlife viewing, stay on the designated trails and use a good set of binoculars. The salt marsh is truly a fragile place and access into it is definitely not allowed. Besides crushing the vegetation and scaring the birds, you will leave footprints in the soft mud that may stay visible for many years. Enjoy it from a sensible distance.

*Spencer Spit in summer*

## 12. Weeks Wetland Preserve

**Size and Ownership:** 22 acres (San Juan County Land Bank.)

**Facilities:** Trail, viewing platform. [No camping, toilets or bicycles on trail.] Dogs must be kept on a leash.

**Access:** From the ferry terminal on Lopez Island, travel south on Ferry Road for about 2 miles, bearing right at the junction with Center Road. At this point the road becomes known as Fisherman Bay Road. Continue on this road for another two miles, turning right onto Lopez Road, which leads into Lopez Village. Weeks Point Road is on the left. A special parking area for cars has not been provided, so you may wish to park in the village and walk the last little bit. The entry to the short trail leading to the viewing platform is only about 100 yards down the road.

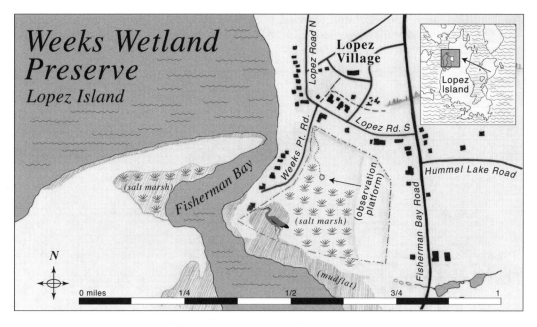

Weeks Wetland Preserve is a small estuarine salt marsh, that was "reclaimed" for farming in the late 1800s. The Weeks family, who first homesteaded on Lopez Island in the 1850s, blocked the mouth of this tiny estuary with an earthen berm in an attempt to create more dry land for agriculture. (Settlers often drained wetlands to develop livestock pasturage and for hay production.) Five generations farmed this spot and parts of the surrounding area but eventually the berm became neglected and it slowly eroded away. As tidal flow to the shallow lagoon became reestablished, the salt marsh gradually returned. Remnants of the old fence lines are still visible in the marsh. A mudflat is exposed at low tide.

The Preserve has a good trail that terminates at a viewing platform complete with bench seats and interpretive signs. A couple of interesting salt marsh plants that grow here include the salty-tasting pickleweed [also called "chicken-feet" because of their resemblance] (*Salicornia virginica*) and saltmarsh dodder (*Cuscuta salina*), a parasite of *Salicornia* whose intertwining stems often look like tangles of orange-colored thread.

Henderson's checker mallow (*Sidalcea hendersonii*), a regional endemic marsh-plant with lovely deep pink-colored petals, can be seen blooming near the edge of the tidelands from June through August. Please do not walk in the marsh, the vegetation is very fragile and can be easily crushed underfoot.

There is often good birdwatching in the surrounding hedgerows of old apple trees, willows, Himalayan blackberry, and Nootka rose. A few of the birds commonly viewed around this site include the northwest crow, red-winged blackbird, common yellowthroat, goldfinch, white-crowned sparrow, song sparrow, savannah sparrow and the occasional yellow warbler. Canada geese and great blue herons are often seen out in the estuary.

*Weeks Wetland Preserve at low tide*

# 13. Fisherman Bay Salt Marsh

**Size and Ownership:** 5+ acres (San Juan County Land Bank.)

**Facilities:** Parking area. [No camping, fires, or drinking water.]

**Access:** From the ferry terminal on Lopez Island, go south on Ferry Road for about 2 miles, bearing right at the junction with Center Road. At this point the road becomes known as Fisherman Bay Road. Continue on this road for another 3.75 miles, turning right onto Bayshore Road, which leads onto a narrow "neck" of land with water on both sides. Park vehicle at Otis Perkins Park (0.5 acre) near the beach. *By boat:* There is a gravel beach suitable for landing kayaks and dinghies at Otis Perkins Park (day use only).

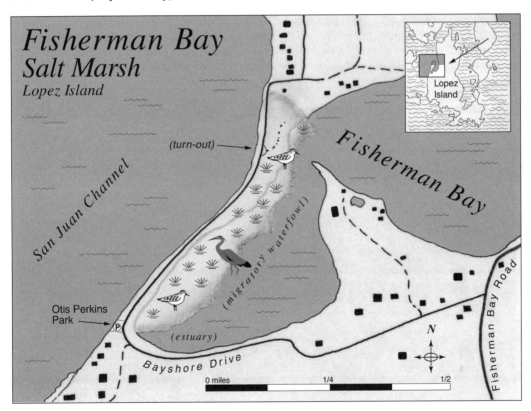

**Fisherman Bay Preserve** was created by the San Juan County Land Bank to protect the significant and particularly fragile salt marsh lagoon located at the head of Fisherman Bay. Because it is so vulnerable to damaging footsteps there are no trails leading into this wetland. (If you try and walk out there you are likely to become

61

mired in hip-deep black mud.)  Anyway, the best viewing is attained by walking the road that runs on top of the narrow neck that separates open water from the bay.

During low tide, much of this sensitive biological area becomes an exposed mudflat.  At high tide, the water is but a few feet deep.  Seashore saltgrass (*Distichlis spicata*) and pickleweed (*Salicornia virginica*) dominate the adjacent salt marsh. Scattered patches of Puget Sound gumweed (*Grindelia integrifolia*) growing on the shoulders of the road brighten the scene with their yellow flowers.  The flower disk, which is actually a composite of many small flowers, is often covered with a sticky resinous gum.  This gum possesses antibiotic properties and was used by the regional natives as a medicine.

Birdwatching for waterfowl and shorebirds is good here, especially during migration periods.  Watch for great blue herons, ducks of many species (including scoters on the seaward side), Heermann's gulls, horned grebes, pectoral sandpipers, yellowlegs, dowitchers, plovers, and ospreys - just to name a few.  Because the shore-line on the seaward side of the road has public access, you might want to wander along its driftwood-scattered cobble beach on your way back to Otis Perkins Park.

*Fisherman Bay Salt Marsh*

# 14. Hummel Lake Preserve

**Size and Ownership:** 79+ acres (San Juan County Land Bank.)

**Facilities:** Trails, boat dock, toilets near parking area. [No fires, camping or drinking water.] Dogs must be kept on a leash. No bicycles on trails.

**Access:** From the ferry terminal on Lopez Island, travel south on Ferry Road for about 2 miles, bearing left onto Center Road at the junction. Continue south along Center Road for another 2 miles and you will see Hummel Lake on your left. The entrance lane to Hummel Lake Preserve is on your left, just south of the lake.

This charming preserve was created from the remnants of an old homestead. Importantly, it conserves a large section of Hummel Lake's southern shoreline and its peripheral wetland. A popular fishing spot, this shallow 35+ acre lake is stocked with large-mouth bass, channel catfish, rainbow trout, and sunfish. (There is a state-owned public access and rowboat launching area at the junction where Center Road and Hummel Lake Road meet. Use of motorboats is prohibited on this lake.)

From within the preserve, access to the lake is by trail leading from the parking area and ending at a small dock. Along the boardwalk that goes out to this dock, you can see the "banding" (zonation) of vegetation created by increasingly wetter soils. Firs and cedars give way to alders, which then give way to willows (*Salix sp.*), then a band of cattails, and finally, a zone of native yellow pond lilies. If you were to look down on this lake from high in the air, you would see what appears to be concentric circles of vegetation types encircling large portions of the lake, especially along this southern shore.

Marshbirds can be spotted from the dock or while walking along Center Road. Osprey, great blue herons, marsh wrens, red-winged blackbirds are common here. In summer, dozens of barn swallows skim over the water's surface, splashing down now and then in a game of "touch and go" that may be the result of grabbing a quick drink or to snap up some emerging aquatic insect. In winter, trumpeter swans are sometimes seen on the lake.

*Vegetatitive zonation at Hummel Lake*

# 15. Shark Reef Park

**Size and Ownership:** 39 acres (San Juan County Park.)

**Facilities:** Trails, picnic tables, and toilets near parking area. [No fires, camping or drinking water.] No bicycles on trails. Dogs must be kept on leashes.

**Access:** From the ferry terminal on Lopez Island, go south on Ferry Road for about 2 miles, bearing right at the junction with Center Road. At this point the road becomes known as Fisherman Bay Road. Continue on this road for another 5 miles, turning right onto Airport Road, then after about half a mile, turn left onto Shark Reef Road. The parking area at the trailhead is on the right about 1.8 miles down Shark Reef Road. *By boat:* There is a small gravelly beach in the little bay just south of Kings Point that is suitable for landing kayaks and dinghies.

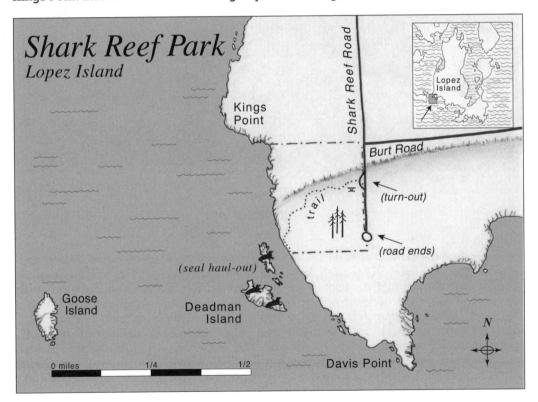

Formerly a U.S. Military Reserve, then a Washington State DNR Recreation Area, and now a County Park, **Shark Reef Park** offers the best land-based viewing of an active harbor seal (*Phoca vitulina*) haulout within the region. Up to 100 seals can often be seen basking on the broken rocky islets just offshore from the park. Here the visitor does not need to worry about concealing him or herself because the seals are completely habituated to non-threatening human presence. I have sat on top of the park's rocky shoreline bluff with a good pair of binoculars and watched the uninhibited behavior of these seals for hours. A squabble here, a youngster having trouble getting back on land, one with too large a fish... it can be fascinating stuff.

*Harbor seals at rest*

Often the largest concentrations of animals will be seen at low tide when there is more rock exposed. (The need to haul out and warm up is critical for these seals.) During periods of high tide, harbor seals usually leave their haul-out spots and swim out to their favorite fishing areas. They are said to be able to dive to three hundred feet and remain submerged for up to 18 minutes, but their usual time underwater appears to range from just 3 to 5 minutes. These seals primarily feed on various bottomfish, including rockfishes, flounders, cod, sculpins and pollock. But they also catch salmon and octopus in summer and squid in winter. Since receiving federal protection in 1972, seal populations within the region have risen rapidly and now may be nearing the "carrying-capacity" for the Salish Sea.

The rocky viewing bluffs can be reached in about 10 to 15 minutes time via a walking trail that leads through the woods from the parking area. Along the way, look for chickadees, nuthatches, eagles, juncos and some really big banana slugs.

## 16. Watmough Bay

**Size and Ownership:** ±8.5 acres (San Juan County Land Bank and BLM.)

**Facilities:** Trail and toilets near parking area. [No fires, camping or drinking water.] Dogs must be kept on leashes at all times.

**Access:** From the ferry terminal on Lopez Island, travel south on Ferry Road for about 2 miles, bearing left onto Center Road at the junction. Continue south along Center Road for 5.5 miles, turning left at the "T" intersection onto Mud Bay Road. Continue on Mud Bay Road for 4.25 miles, turning right onto Watmough Head Road. Pavement soon ends and the road takes a hard left. (Watmough Bay Reserve is 1.4 miles from Mud Bay Road). *By boat:* There is a protected landing beach for kayaks and dinghies at the head of Watmough Bay.

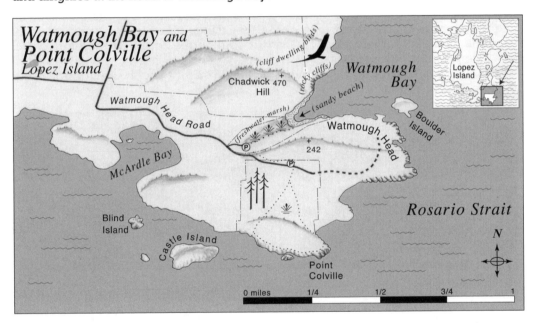

## 17. Point Colville

**Size and Ownership:** 60 acres (Bureau of Land Management.)

**Facilities:** Trails. Parking just off dirt road. [No fires, camping, or drinking water.] No bikes on trails. Pets must be kept on leashes.

**Access:** Same as for Watmough Bay but continue on past Watmough Bay turnoff for approximately 0.35 mile. Trailhead is not obvious but is located to the right shortly before reaching the gate at end of road. *By boat:* Not recommended.

**Watmough Bay Preserve** is located on the southeast end of Lopez Island. The preserve began in 1993 when a small stretch of beach was donated to the San Juan County Land Bank. Realizing the fragility of the area and the neccessity of protecting it, the Land Bank later negotiated a conservation easement with BLM on about eight adjoining acres of freshwater wetland and beach.

The beach at the head of the bay is open to public use but the dense growth of cattails in the adjacent marsh restricts access to just its periphery. Red-winged blackbirds, marsh wrens, mink and river otter are common residents of this wetland, which has no visible outlet stream. Apparently, surplus water infiltrates downward through the gravel berm at the top of the beach and out into Watmough Bay. (Most likely, this marsh was originally a saltwater lagoon that eventually became isolated by the slow buildup of gravel, sand, and other beach material.)

The trail from the parking area is rather dark and close but when you step out into the open near the beach, one of the first things you become aware of is the grandeur of the high sheer cliffs of Chadwick Hill to the north. These rugged rock faces support both peregrine falcon and turkey vulture nesting sites. If you watch carefully during late spring and summer months, you may see the adult birds bringing food to their young.

*A shaft of evening sun illuminates the beach at Watmough Bay*

**Point Colville** is a BLM-managed Lighthouse Reserve. (The lighthouse has never been built and fortunately the land has remained in public ownership.) It is now managed as an "area of critical environmental concern" (ACEC).

Parking is on the north of the road and the trailhead is not clearly marked. The trail wanders through an area of mature forest that includes white fir, western hemlock, some very big Douglas fir specimens, western red cedar, and shore pine. This is an excellent deep forest experience, often with an open and park-like mossy floor highlighted by brushy patches of the glossy-leaved salal.

The trail winds around a large forested wetland dominated by Sitka spruce and red alder with an understory of sword ferns and sedges. An unusual plant called the leathery grape-fern (*Botrychium multifidum*) can occasionally be found growing in this area.

Eventually the trail passes through a patch of "dog-hair" thicket (a dense stand of small trees) and out onto an open rocky bluff with the sea below. Here the shore pines and madronas have been stunted by a combination of poor soil and harsh salt-laden winter winds. Native grasses (*Festuca*) and Puget Sound gumweed dominate the thin soils of this wild area beyond the tree zone.

*Castle Island seen from the cliffs at Point Colville*

69

## 18. Iceberg Island

**Size and Ownership:** 3.25 acres (State Land managed by Washington State Parks.)

**Facilities:** None. [No fires, camping, or drinking water.] No pets.

**Access:** *By boat:* Iceberg Island is located about 0.4 nautical mile northeast of Iceberg Point. Since the shoreline is very steep and rocky, the only potential landing sites are two tiny rocky inlets on either side of the south end of the island.

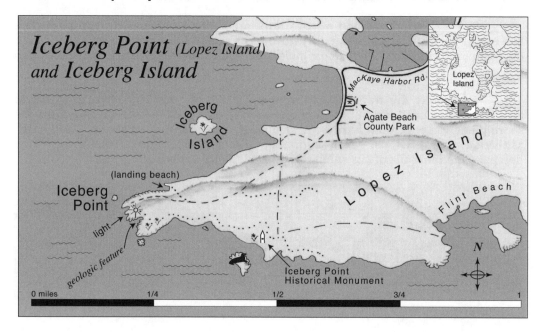

*Iceberg Point (Lopez Island) and Iceberg Island*

## 19. Iceberg Point

**Size and Ownership:** 85 acres (Federal: Administered by BLM and USCG.)

**Facilities:** Tracks and trails. [No fires, camping, or drinking water.] No bicycles on trails. Pets must be kept on leashes at all times.

**Access:** From the ferry terminal on Lopez Island, travel south on Ferry Road for about 2 miles, bearing left onto Center Road at the junction. Continue south on Center Road for 5.5 miles, turning left at the "T" intersection onto Mud Bay Road. Continue on Mud Bay Road for 2.8 miles, turning right onto Mackaye Harbor Road and continue to end of road. *By boat:* There is a gravelly beach suitable for landing kayaks and dinghies located in a small cove just northeast of the light on Iceberg Point. A steep trail leads from the beach to top of the bluff

**Iceberg Island** is located about halfway between Iceberg Point and Agate Beach. Because the island is rather barren and offers no good landing beaches or mooring spots, it receives very few visitors. Depending on the state of the tide and which way the wind is blowing, the best landing sites on the island are usually one of two small rocky inlets located on either side of the south end of the island. Once you have made it safely ashore, however, it may be a good idea to haul out your dinghy or kayak and stow it above the high tide zone because there is a good chance of it getting battered by the occasional breaking wave.

The southern lobe of this small island has an excellent rocky intertidal zone. During periods of low tide, several lovely tidepools complete with small shrimp, green anemones, sculpins, periwinkles and limpets are revealed. Goose-necked barnacles and mussels can be seen above the tidepools in the littoral zone.

*Spring wildflowers and* Sedum lanceolatum *mantle the bare rock of Iceberg Island*

Although the island is treeless, its central portion is vegetated with native grasses, Puget Sound gumweed, gold-backed fern, Pacific cinquefoil, camas, and very large specimens of miner's lettuce (*Montia perfoliata*). Some of the miner's lettuce leaf shields are up to 3 inches in diameter. (This is probably due to soil enrichment from guano from the numerous double-crested cormorants and nesting Canada geese that frequent the island.) During April and May, much of this island is blanketed by an intense display of flowering sea blush, lance-leafed sedum and large patches of shooting stars. (The spring show of pink-flowering sea blush (*Plectritis congesta*) is the best that I've ever seen.) **If you land on this island, please be very careful where you step so you do not crush these sensitive plants.**

The north end of the island is thickly covered with low growing wild rose and rank growths of weeds and grasses. (Watch for river otters here.) By late spring most of the flowers will have withered and set seed leaving behind just the tougher grasses and shrubs.

**Iceberg Point** is a beautifully rugged part of Lopez Island. Whenever I visit this austere landscape, I imagine what this entire region might have looked like some 200 years ago when European settlement began. But if you are a careful observer, you will also see a few of the examples of "deep time" that exist here as well.

*Iceberg Point*

One of the most dramatic instances occurs just east of the navigation light, which supports red triangular-shaped daymarks. Here a short steep "gully" opens to the sea. If you look carefully at the rock face on either side of that gully, you will see that it has been polished by glacial scouring. This "scouring" occurred some 14 to 17,000 years ago during the last great Ice Age when a glacier consisting of many millions of tons of ice (up to a mile thick) covered this landscape.

The contact point between the ice of a glacier and the underlying bedrock is not static; the ice (under great pressure from sheer mass) is constantly moving. In many ways, it is useful to think of a glacier as a one-way conveyor belt of slowly moving ice. As new ice is added to the top end, the "old" ice at the lower end crumbles or melts away.

You can actually see the direction of this glacier's travel towards the south by examining the rockface for scratches (striations) created by the sandpaper effect of the innumerable bits of rock, sand and silt that were trapped between the two surfaces of rock and ice. Iceberg Point was so named by the United States Coast Survey of 1854 because of these "remarkably deep and smooth marks of glacial action."

If you hike out to Iceberg Point from the end of Mackaye Harbor Road, please be aware that the access track is provided courtesy of the owners of the surrounding private lands. Parking is very limited at the trailhead, so to avoid congestion I usually park my vehicle at nearby Agate Beach County Park and walk from there.

In 1991, the Bureau of Land Management designated Iceberg Point as an "area of critical environmental concern" (ACEC) in order to protect the natural values of this site, particularly the wildflowers which include the rare California buttercup (*Ranunculus californicus*) and brittle cactus (*Opuntia fragilis*).

The overall ecology of this site is rather complicated but it is primarily influenced by the thin covering of soils which overlay the bedrock. Rocky balds and miniature grassland prairies have been created in places where the soil is too thin to support woody vegetation. Inland, the deeper soils support mixed conifer forest. It is this coastal rocky bald/prairie complex that sustains the vast majority of the area's spring wildflowers such as naked desert parsley, camas, sea thrift, Puget Sound gumweed, seaside lupine, chocolate lily, Hooker's onion, and spring gold. During a good year these species can create stunning wildflower displays.

When visiting the area, you are asked to stay on the trails (which are open to foot traffic only), keep your dog on a leash at all times and to pack out any litter.

# 20. Squaw Bay Headland

**Size and Ownership:** 40.25 acres [Out of total of 59.75 acres comprising the Shaw Island County Park.] (San Juan County Parks.)

**Facilities:** Shoreline car track. Camping, drinking water, and toilets in nearby developed section of park. [Pets must be kept on leashes.]

**Access:** From the ferry dock go south on Blind Bay Road for 1.25 miles, turning left onto Squaw Bay Road. Continue along Squaw Bay Road for about a mile; the track to Squaw Bay Headland is off to the left just as Squaw Bay comes into view.
*By boat:* There is a nice "pocket beach" suitable for landing kayaks and dinghies located at the entrance to Squaw Bay just east of a small rocky point. The shoreline east of this little cove is on private property. Please respect it.

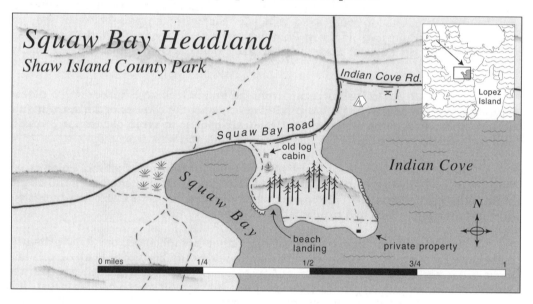

**Squaw Bay Headland** is primarily an undeveloped section of Shaw Island County Park. However, its entire southern end is private land and not open to public access. (Note line east of beach landing site on above map.) Formerly an abandoned military reservation, the public portion of this area was granted to San Juan County for $250 in 1927 "for recreational public-park purposes" by an act of Congress.

The headland's primary vegetative cover is a tall mixed transitional forest containing scattered individuals of large old-growth Douglas fir. The forest floor provides excellent mushrooming in autumn and fine displays of calypso orchids (*Calypso bulbosa*) can been seen in mid-spring. While there are no formal walking paths on this property, numerous deer trails braid through the forest. There is also a long private driveway easement that bisects the eastern third of the property to allow local access to the house at the tip of the headland.

Just off the dirt track that runs along the shore of Squaw Bay sits the remains of a log cabin. According to several longtime residents, this building was used as Shaw Island's first school house. The roof has now collapsed and its carefully notched logs are slowly subsiding back into ecology of the forest. Near here, the tree cover opens up enough to support a grassy understory. In the 1890s this area was cleared pasture.

*A log deposited by a receding tide balances precariously
on the rocky shore of Squaw Bay Headland*

The Squaw Bay car track terminates near a grassy bald on the west side of the headland. A foot-path leads down to the landing beach mentioned earlier. Some of the wildlife to watch for while visiting this area include river otters, mink, bald eagles, belted kingfishers, black-tailed deer, pileated woodpeckers, Canada geese, and ravens.

# Part 4: ORCAS ISLAND

    *Unlike the popular belief, Orcas Island did not receive its name from the toothed whale (the Orca) that our region is so famous for. Instead, it appears to be a contraction of the name bestowed in 1791 by Spanish explorer Francisco de Eliza to honor the Viceroy of Mexico, Don Juan Vincente de Guemes Pacheco Padilla Horcasitas y Aguayo Conde de Revilla Gigedo, who was patron of his expedition. (The Spanish laid claim to all of the San Juan Islands until 1795 when Spain agreed to abandon her interests north of California.)*

    *When viewed on a map, Orcas Island resembles a pair of misshapen saddlebags thrown over the top of Eastsound. The largest island in the San Juan archipelago, covering nearly 57 square miles, it is served daily by Washington State Ferries and charter flight services. With a resident population of more than 5,000 people, there is a full range of tourist accommodations available to visitors to the island.*

    *Of the 14 natural areas described in this section, five of them (Victim Island, Skull Island, Freeman Island, Lawrence Point, and Point Doughty) are only accessible by private boat or kayak. Campsites can be found (when available) at popular Moran State Park and at (hike-in only) Obstruction Pass State Park. Call the Moran State Park office at (360) 376-2326 to determine campsite availability and to make reservations.*

# 21. Cayou Lagoon

**Size and Ownership:** ±15 acres (Private, with upland conservation easements.)

**Facilities:** None. [Viewing from road and bridge only.]

**Access:** From the ferry dock at Orcas Landing, turn left and drive north on Horseshoe Highway for 2.6 miles, turning left onto Deer Harbor Road. Continue along shoreline for another 4.6 miles, turning right onto Channel Road. Stop near the little wooden bridge at bottom of hill.

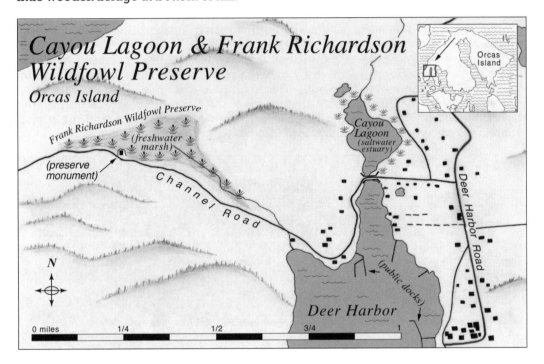

# 22. Frank Richardson Wildfowl Preserve

**Size and Ownership:** ± 26.5 acres (Private, with conservation easements.)

**Facilities:** None. [Viewing from road only.]

**Access:** From bridge at Cayou Lagoon continue on for 0.8 mile along Channel Road. Preserve marshland is on right side of road.

**Cayou Lagoon** is best viewed from the little bridge where Channel Road crosses the narrow channel that alternately fills and empties the lagoon with each major tide. The lagoon is named after Louis Cayou, an early settler who homesteaded a small farm and grazed stock on the lush marsh grasses here during the late 1800s.

At low tide the lagoon empties, revealing a broad mudflat. During this time, great blue herons are often seen stalking shallow pools for small fish trapped by the receding water. During certain seasons (and tides) many herons can be attracted to this site. A few years ago, in an amazing spectacle, I counted nearly thirty of these big birds scattered across the exposed flat.

When the tide turns and water begins racing along the channel under the bridge to refill the lagoon again, look carefully into the stream. You will very likely glimpse part of the horde of little fishes that reenter the lagoon during high tide. Some of these schools of fish flash by in seemingly endless lines, especially during the period between mid to high tide. This is graphic evidence of the productivity of this small estuary. Other wildlife that frequent the lagoon include raccoons, river otters, black-tailed deer, belted kingfishers, ospreys, mergansers, and the various shorebirds who visit the mudflats at low tide.

*Cayou Lagoon*

The **Frank Richardson Wildfowl Preserve** is a large freshwater marsh that was accidentally created when the culvert that drained this wetland (for agricultural purposes) became plugged up many years ago. (The remains of old fence posts can still be seen standing in the water.) In 1994 the San Juan Preservation Trust formalized the preserve, naming it in honor of Dr. Frank Richardson, a retired University of Washington professor, who was an enthusiastic supporter of the marsh.

There is no public access to the preserve but many of the birds can easily be viewed from the road, using the fringing shrubbery as a screen. Just past the 1-mile marker on the right, you'll see a large rock that bears a memorial plaque and an area wide enough to park off the road.

The marsh teems with bird life. Species commonly seen here are the marsh wren, Brewer's and red-winged blackbird, sora, Virginia rail, bufflehead duck, Canada goose, great blue heron, pied-billed grebe, hooded merganser, mallard duck, fox sparrow, and many others. During the autumn migration season, I've observed flocks of ducks that numbered in the hundreds.

*Part of the wetlands of the Frank Richardson Wildfowl Preserve*

Although the Frank Richardson Wildfowl Preserve and Cayou Lagoon appear to be two separate sites, they are connected by a wildlife corridor formed by a stream gully and several small ponds on private property. Both areas are protected under a system of private conservation easements. Of these conscientious property owners, Bob and Meg Connor are the outstanding stewards of Cayou Lagoon and much of the land that surrounds it, including the wildlife corridor to Frank Richardson Wildfowl Preserve. In recent years they have facilitated an assortment of environmental research and restoration projects here with a variety of organizations that includes Ducks Unlimited, the NRCS, the Dept. of Agriculture, Western Washington State University, and several local public schools. Permission to tour these projects can be arranged by telephoning the Connors at (360) 376-2480.

*A black-tailed deer stands in tall summer grass*

## 23. Skull Island

**Size and Ownership:** 2.5 acres (Bureau of Land Management.)

**Facilities:** None. [No camping or fires.] Dogs must be kept on leashes.

**Access:** *By boat:* Situated near the north end of Massacre Bay on West Sound, there are two small shell beaches located on the east side of the island that are suitable for landing kayaks and dinghies. These beaches only appear during low tide; during higher water you'll have to wait or take your chances by landing on the rocks. The nearest public launch point for paddle boats is the County Dock located at the head of Massacre Bay near the intersection of Deer Harbor Road and Crow Valley Road.

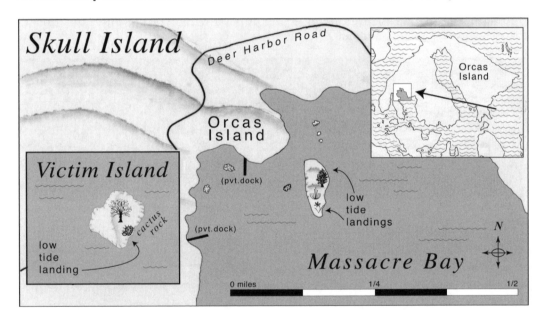

## 24. Victim Island

**Size and Ownership:** 4 acres (Bureau of Land Management.)

**Facilities:** None. [No camping or fires.] Dogs must be kept on leashes.

**Access:** *By boat:* Located on the west side of West Sound (1.7 miles South East of Skull Island) there is small landing beach on the southeast side of the island that appears during low tide. The nearest public launch point for paddle boaters heading to this island is also the County Dock located at the head of Massacre Bay.

For many years **Skull Island** was managed by Washington State Parks but that contract was allowed to expire and now BLM is responsible for its administration. Fortunately for the island's ecology, Parks did not develop the island by installing a dock or building a campground. Consequently, the island has remained in almost pristine condition. The name comes from a human skull that was found on the island in the 1800s. Apparently, some of these small islands were used as cemeteries by indigenous people.

Although it is complicated by various micro-habitats, I generally classify the island's vegetation as a juniper and grassland savannah. The dominant tree cover, Rocky Mountain juniper (*Juniperus scopulorum*), is a disjunct species restricted in western Washington to the San Juan Islands and the Gulf Islands of southern British Columbia. Other native plants that make up this rocky savannah include Idaho and red fescue, Puget Sound gumweed, and Hooker's onion. River otter and Canada geese are seasonally common.

*Rocky Mountain junipers frame the view from Skull Island*

**Victim Island** was also formerly managed by Washington State Parks with BLM now responsible for its administration. I am not certain on how the island got its name, but it appears to reflect a grim event in history.

The island's geology is composed of a mixture of Orcas chert and sandstone with an overlay of glacial till. Maximum altitude is about 60 feet with a rather steep rocky shore all around the island.

Victim Island supports a rather dense forest consisting of a mixture of Pacific madronas, some Rocky Mountain junipers, old and young Douglas firs, and a few Garry oaks, which are scattered across the island. Shrubby understory consists primarily of ocean spray. The most significant botanical feature on this island is a large colony of brittle cactus (*Opuntia fragilis*) on top of a rocky "shoulder" on the southeastern end of the island.

*Victim Island seen from the west*

85

## 25. Killebrew Lake

**Size and Ownership:** 145 acres including the 31 acre lake  (State Land managed by Washington State Department of Fish and Wildlife.)

**Facilities:** Trail, public float, no drinking water or toilets. [Area closed during hours of darkness, no camping or fires.] Pets must be kept on leashes.

**Access:** Killibrew Lake is located 2.4 miles from Orcas Island Ferry Terminal via Killebrew Lake Road.  To access float and off-road parking continue on past White Beach Road for  about 0.1 mile (the road turns to gravel) and turn onto the dirt drive at the first left.

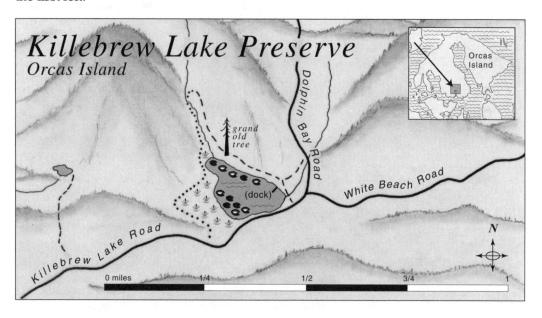

Killebrew Lake is an excellent example of an older, rather eutrophic, lowland lake occupying a depression formed by the surrounding hills.  The attractive centerpiece of the entire preserve, this lake supports a large freshwater marsh that now occupies much of the lake's former western lobe.  Yellow pond-lilies fringe the lake's clear open waters  to the north and along much of its southeast side.

Judging from the lake's geologic history, it will likely fill with self-generated peat within the next 450 to 650 years.  However, it is this transitional phase of open water to marsh and bog that makes this small basin an important repository of bio-diversity.  Botanists have already recorded the presence of two rare plants living in the marsh and more are likely to appear as the marshes and bogs increase in size.

Positioned near an abandoned house is a 60-foot-long float dock where small boats can be hand-carried for launching (gasoline motors not permitted). The lake is said to have been stocked with cutthroat trout and large-mouth bass in years past and at present certainly contains pumpkinseed sunfish and bullfrogs. Other wildlife regularly observed here include pied-billed grebe, sora, Virginia rail, belted kingfisher, osprey and bald eagle. The lake's nearshore zone supports a mixed community of rushes, skunk cabbage, willows, thimbleberry, wild roses, evergreen blackberries, red alder, western red cedar and Douglas fir.

An old quarry road leading north past the deserted house offers peek-a-boo views of the lake. Along this track stands a very large Douglas fir (6.2 ft. dbh & 114 ft. high). Look for bald eagles perched on its top. At the end of the track, a trail dips down into a gully filled with fern-covered quarry boulders and then climbs along the hill bordering the western side of the lake. Near the head of the lake, this trail offers a good view of a fine cedar and alder-forested wetland.

Climbing through dry second-growth forest to an elevation about 200 feet above the lake, the trail eventually leads back down towards water. Nice patches of Indian pipe, Steller's jays, chestnut-backed chickadees, and little piles of chewed fir-cones left by Douglas squirrels can be seen along this section of trail in summer. When the trail comes out onto an old drive turn downhill to the left. The track emerges southwest of the lake onto Killebrew Lake Road right next to the 2-mile marker. You can complete the 1.5 mile-long loop around the lake by walking back along this paved road to your starting point.

*Killebrew Lake*

## 26. Point Doughty

**Size and Ownership:** ± 4 acres (State Land managed by Washington State Parks.)

**Facilities:** Picnic tables, pit toilets. Primitive campsite, no drinking water.] No dogs.

**Access:** *By boat:* There are no amenities for boats but kayaks and dinghies can be landed in a small cove located on the south side of the point.

## 27. Freeman Island

**Size and Ownership:** 0.83 acre (Bureau of Land Management.)

**Facilities:** None. [No camping, fires, or pets.]

**Access:** *By boat:* There are no amenities for boats but kayaks and dinghies can be landed on the southeastern shore of this rocky island during mid-to-low tides.

The northern shoreline of **Point Doughty** is defined by precipitous cliffs while its more sheltered southern shore is characterized by rock outcrops and gravelly beaches. Because of resident bald eagles and other natural values, the entire 51 acre point has been designated by the Washington Department of Natural Resources as a "Natural Area Preserve" (NAP). While this would usually mean that such an area would be closed to the general public, the State has shown unusual leniency by continuing to allow camping on the open grassy portion of the point. The rest of the point is closed to public access.

*The rocky cliff on the north side of Point Doughty*

**Freeman Island** is a narrow rocky ridge of land jutting out of the water. Barely 500 feet long, it is located about a mile south of the tip of Point Doughty. For many years this island was designated as a Washington State Marine Park but the role of administration has now been returned to the BLM.

This is another bit of natural land that has benefited from a lack of management and/or development. Essentially just an eroded ridge, it manages to support about 25-30 trees and large shrubs including a few Rocky Mountain junipers and several large specimens of western serviceberry (*Amelanchier alnifolia* var. *semiintegrifolia*). Canada geese often nest in summer on the small grassy area located on the western end of the island. In spring, a fine display of white fawn-lily (*Erythronium oregonum*) often blooms in this same grassy spot. Bald eagles are often seen perching on one or two of the island's larger trees. Excellent examples of honeycomb eroded sandstone can be found near the tide line on the south shore.

Freeman Island and honeycomb eroded sandstone (below)

## 28. Madrona Point

**Size and Ownership:** 23.6 acres (Lummi Indian Tribe.)

**Facilities:** Trails. [No camping, fires, dogs, bikes, or drinking water.]

**Access:** From the ferry dock at Orcas Landing, head for the village of Eastsound and turn south onto Prune Alley. There is an area for parking at its end. *By boat:* There is a public dock near the parking area.

## 29. Crescent Beach Marsh

**Size and Ownership:** ±23 acres (+7 acres San Juan Preservation Trust, ±16 acres San Juan County Land Bank.)

**Facilities:** None. [Viewing from parking turnout only.]

**Access:** Continue east from the village of Eastsound along Crescent Beach Drive. Parking turnout is about a half mile from town. *By boat:* Crescent Beach offers a good landing for kayaks and dinghies. Stay clear of the oyster farm that occupies the west half of beach.

**Madrona Point** contains one of the most significant publicly accessed groves of Pacific madrona (*Abutus menziesii*) in San Juan County. (There are very few places in Washington State where madronas occur in pure stands such as this.) Couple these elegant smooth-barked trees with a rugged rocky peninsula indented with tiny "pocket beaches" and you have a place of exceptional beauty.

Although Madrona Point is the property of the Lummi Indian Nation (it was a native burial site prior to European settlement), it is open to visitors during daylight hours. People coming by boat can tie up at the Madrona Point County Dock, which is conveniently located less than 150 feet from the trail head.

Soon after striking out for the point, you will quickly discover that the main trail branches out into a network of smaller "casual" trails that sometimes lead to unexpected and lovely places. For example, near the outer end of the point are discrete little areas that are sometimes covered with a profusion of wildflowers in the spring. In these interstices between the rocks, I have found masses of great camas, showy chickweed, naked desert parsley, spring gold, death camas, Henderson's shooting star, and a rare patch or two of the ephemeral large-flowered blue-eyed Mary (*Collinsia grandiflora*).

*The twisted skeleton of a juniper overhangs a bluff*

Some of the madronas along the bluff on the point's western shore have been sculpted and stunted into mere hedges by the strong winds that blast up through Eastsound during winter and early spring.  It is a hard life here on the weather side; several of the trees have been half-killed by the salt spray, while others have already been reduced to sunbleached woody skeletons.

A bit of the wildlife commonly seen here include black-tailed deer, river otter, bald eagles, white-crowned sparrows and rufous-sided towhees.  At low tide this is a great place to explore tide pools and to marvel over the large bright orange-colored piaster starfish clinging to the exposed rocks.

**Crescent Beach Marsh** contains the most significant grove of quaking aspen (*Populus tremuloides*) in the San Juan Islands.  Formerly a salt marsh, this area was inadvertently transformed into a freshwater wetland when the road berm for Crescent Beach Drive was created in the early 1900s.  Cut off from direct tidal influence, the marsh was slowly leached of it's soil salts, allowing the aspens to become established.  (This unique area has now been protected in a preserve created by the San Juan County Land Bank and the San Juan Preservation Trust.)

*Aspens at Crescent Beach Marsh*

There's a parking turnoff next to the grove where you can have a close look at this unusual "island" variety of quaking aspen.  They can grow much larger than most aspens, one specimen here measured over 24 inches in diameter and 70 feet tall.

# 30. The Four Falls Area

**Size and Ownership:** Approximately 1.5 miles of freshwater riparian zone extending from Mountain Lake to the Horseshoe Highway. (Washington State Parks.)

**Facilities:** Public parking, trails. [No camping, fires, toilets, or drinking water.] Dogs must be kept on leashes.

**Access:** From the ferry dock turn left onto the Horseshoe Highway and continue

Four Falls
Moran State Park, Orcas Island

2032
+ Little Summit

Orcas Island

Mountain Lake

boat ramp

Mountain Lake Rd.

Paul Creek

Mount Constitution Road

Hidden Falls

Cascade Creek

P

Cavern Falls

Rustic Falls

Cascade Falls

HORSESHOE HWY

trail to Cascade Lake
and campground

N

0 miles   1/4   1/2   3/4   1

along this road through the village of Eastsound (5.6 miles) into Moran State Park, turning left at the junction with Mount Constitution Road (14 miles from the ferry dock). A parking area is located on the right, 0.4 miles after leaving the Horseshoe Highway. A short spur trail leads down to Cascade Falls and Cascade Creek where it joins a longer trail that follows the creek all the way from Cascade Lake to Mountain Lake. Both trails are heavily used in summer.

**Cascade Creek** has created the largest and most diverse riparian habitat in the San Juan Islands Archipelago. Most visitors, however, only come to see the several falls, especially Cascade Falls, which can be quite impressive during periods of high water in spring and early summer. These falls are fed year-round by Cascade Creek, flowing down from Mountain Lake. Winding its way through mixed coniferous forest with occasional large specimens of old growth Douglas fir scattered here and there, this crystal-clear little stream is the true ecological wealth of the area. It supports a wide variety of wildlife, including water striders, mayflies, eastern brook trout, belted kingfishers, muskrats, and raccoons.

*Cascade Falls in spring flow*

A miniature of the much larger mainland riparian systems like the Skagit and Snohomish Rivers, Cascade Creek is complete with log jams, undercut banks, and is often edged by an understory mosaic of salmonberry bushes and sword ferns. Here and there, shade-tolerant western hemlock saplings can be seen coming up under the older trees. Like its larger cousins, this little ecosystem goes through a yearly cycle of winter flood and summer ebb.

This stream is the only location where I have regularly seen water ouzels (*Cinclus mexicanus*) in the San Juan Islands. These dull-colored slate-gray birds deserve much more than a passing glance. They exhibit some of the most remarkable behavior of any bird in the region. For starters, their liquid flutelike voice produces the most complicated and entrancing birdsong that I have ever heard. (John Muir was also captivated by this bird's musical talents and waxed lyrically about it in his own writings.) You won't often hear it, though, because the bird usually just makes a monotonous "dzeet, dzeet, dzeet" sound, especially when it knows its being watched.

Also called the American dipper (because of its continual bobbing knee-bending motion) the water ouzel is never far from clear running water. It is capable of both walking underwater along the bottom of a stream and flying through a waterfall. In fact, they often nest behind waterfalls. Over the years, I have discovered several of their round globular mossy nests. Two of them were secreted between the wet rocks in the small space created between the wall and the water of a plunging torrent. Imagine my surprise when I first saw one of these birds exit its nest by darting straight out through a rushing cataract!

As it continues upstream, Cascade Creek trail passes several smaller drops. Moist spray below Rustic Falls supports a particularly lovely grotto of maidenhair fern (*Adiantum pedatum*). When the trail joins Pickett Road (really just a wider track), turn right and follow the road to the top of the next rise. Here, the trail crosses the creek just above Hidden Falls over a log footbridge and then continues upstream until it reaches the dam at Mountain Lake. At this point the trail joins another track that circles the lake shore in both directions.

# 31. Summit Lake

**Size and Ownership:** 12.6 acres (Washington State Parks.)

**Facilities:** Service track from Mount Constitution Road to northern end of lake. [Camping, picnic tables, drinking water, and toilets are available in other areas of the park.] Pets must be kept on leashes.

**Access:** From the ferry dock, turn left onto the Horseshoe Highway and continue along this road through the village of Eastsound (5.6 miles) and on to the junction with Mount Constitution Road (14 miles from the ferry dock). Turn left onto Mount Constitution Road and go another 4.25 miles. (About a mile after negotiating a series of spectacular switchbacks, you will see the lake alongside the road to your right.)

At 2,135 feet above sea level, **Summit Lake** is the highest altitude body of water in the San Juan Islands. It is situated in Moran State Park about 1,100 feet southwest of and just 272 feet below the summit of Mount Constitution, which is the San Juan Archipelago's highest point.

To access the northern end of the lake, there is a pullout near a short service road (leading to a pumping-station) that you use to walk down to the water. Due to its altitude, the surrounding forest (a mixed coniferous woodland containing some majestic hemlocks and an open mossy understory) is noticeably cooler than island forest located closer to sea-level. Look for yellow wild violets scattered in spots over the forest floor. With few bird species other than the occasional chickadee or crow resident in these dense woods, there is often an almost cathedral-like quality to the silence here.

Lying generally in a north/south direction, Summit Lake is approximately two thousand feet long and just 265 feet wide at its broadest point. The outflow for the lake is located on its southeast end. This intermittent stream descends 1,223 feet down to nearby Mountain Lake in a run that is less than a mile long... quite a dramatic drop. Summit Lake's water level is now controlled by a small concrete coffer dam built in the 1940s at the outflow site. The lake's deepest spots are less than 10 feet deep. There are no fish in this lake.

*Rushes and pond lilies in forest-rimmed Summit Lake*

What this shallow marshy lake does have, though, are two very good examples of floating sphagnum bog. Due to increased water depth maintained by the dam, these bogs have formed vegetative islands (one in the north end of the lake and the other in its center) that support a variety of specialized plants including skunk cabbage, swamp laurel, Labrador tea, thread-stemmed cranberry, and the carnivorous broad-leafed sundew (*Drosera rotundifolia*). Although there is no access out onto the floating bogs (they might not support your weight anyway) examples of these interesting plants, including the tiny sundews, can be seen growing in isolated patches along the shores of the lake. Yellow pond lily (*Nuphar polysepalum*) has colonized many of the areas of shallow water ranging from 1.5 to 4 feet deep with a muddy bottom. The seeds of this aquatic plant were once widely used by the native people of this region as a food source.

From May through June (sometimes into July), the most noticeable animal species in the lake is the rough-skinned newt (*Taricha granulosa*) who come here in their hundreds to eat mosquito larvae, mate, and lay eggs. These extremely aquatic 5 to 6-inch-long salamanders are brown-colored on their backs but sport a bright orange or yellow-orange ventral surface. That bright belly apparently serves as warning coloration, for these animals have poisonous skin secretions that effectively repel most would-be predators. Incidentally, it is very a good idea to wash your hands after handling one of these creatures... especially before eating lunch. (This is experienced advice!)

*Rough-skinned newt*

# 32. Lawrence Point

**Size and Ownership:** 109 + acres (State Land.)

**Facilities:** None. [No camping or drinking water.] Pets must be kept on leashes.

**Access:** *By boat:* Lawrence Point is located on the extreme eastern tip of Orcas Island. There are several gravel beaches suitable for landing kayaks and dinghies.

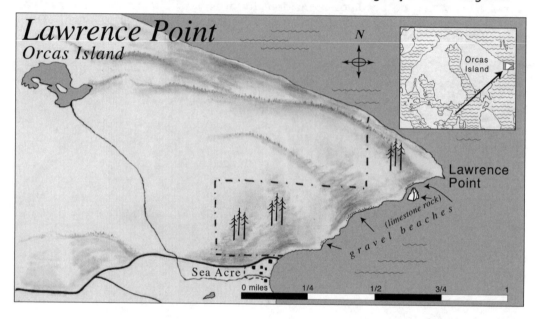

With more than a mile of undeveloped shoreline to explore, **Lawrence Point** is one of the more rugged natural areas in the San Juan Archipelago. A former federal lighthouse reserve, this complex property has remained relatively undisturbed during the past fifty years or so. Unfortunately, the long term future of this lovely area has recently come into question because of changes in state administrative policies.

Access is by small boat, landing onto one of the three sand and gravel "pocket" beaches located along the south shore. (There is no public access from the upland side because one must pass through private lands to reach this property.) A faint trail follows the shoreline but there are no formal paths into the interior.

Historically, this site has been logged at least twice since European settlement. Many of the older tree stumps bear springboard notches, evidence of a logging technique used in the late 1800s and early 1900s. Here and there stand a few old fire-scarred snags but most of this quiet forest consists of tall, mature conifers such as

Douglas fir, western hemlock, shore pine, and some Sitka spuce. There are various large trees with some individuals ranging from 3 to 4.5 feet dbh (diameter breast high). At the time when I did my measurements, several of them exceeded 5 feet in diameter. Many of these were probably left standing because of bends in their trunk and other defects to their marketability.

The forest shrub layer here is most often characterized by a tall understory of ocean spray and (in moister areas) salmonberry. The property also contains several upland rocky bald areas and a small forested wetland about an acre in size that is filled with sedges (*Carex sp.*) and salmonberry shrubs.

Much of the foreshore is steep and rocky, studded with shore pines, junipers, Pacific madrona and Douglas firs. At the top of this embankment, open grassy balds support various wildflowers such as the locally rare Kamchatka lily, fawn lily, camas, and Puget Sound gumweed. Around the point itself occur patches of undisturbed native grasses, such as Idaho fescue, red fescue, and Alaska oniongrass. Commonly seen birds include rose-breasted nuthatches, northern flickers, pileated woodpeckers, downy woodpeckers, dark-eyed juncos, and mountain chickadees.

*The rocky shoreline of Lawrence Point*

# 33. Obstruction Pass State Park

**Size and Ownership:** 80.8 acres (State land managed by Washington States Parks.)

**Facilities:** Trail, picnic tables, campsites, and pit toilets. [No drinking water.] No bicycles on trails. Pets must be kept on leashes.

**Access:** From the Orcas Island ferry dock, follow Orcas Road (Horseshoe Highway) to the town of Eastsound. From Main Street, continue east on Crescent Beach Drive, turning right onto Olga Road (also part of the Horseshoe Highway) to the village of Olga (approximately 16 miles from the ferry dock). Then turn left onto Point Lawrence Road, followed by another right onto Obstruction Pass Road. Watch for Obstruction Pass Park Road on the right. Follow this dirt road to the parking area at its very end. The park's trail to the camping area and the beach begins here.
*By boat:* There is a beach suitable for landing kayaks and dinghies located near the camping area on the west side of the park. It is located about one mile south of Olga.

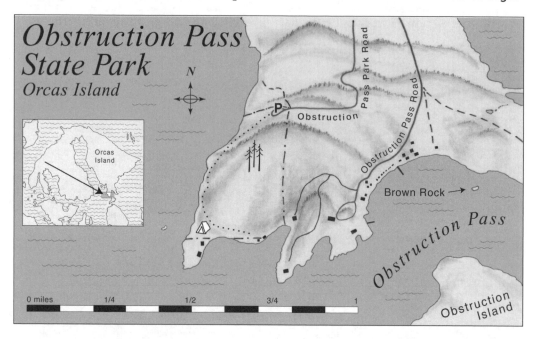

**Obstruction Pass State Park** (a former DNR recreation site) is situated on the western and southwestern slopes of an unnamed 300-foot-high hill fronting East Sound and Obstruction Pass. Apart from a long beach backed by a bluff made of bedrock and glacial till, most of the property supports a mature second growth transitional forest composed mainly of Douglas fir interspersed with a mixture of western red cedar, grand fir, and Pacific madrona (particularly near the edge of the sea bluff). The shrub layer near the bluff is mostly comprised of dense salal, wild rose, and some willow. Inland, it quickly graduates into a very rocky open forest dominated by an ocean spray understory. Glacial striations are evident on some of the exposed rock faces.

Because of its relative seclusion, Obstruction Pass State Park has become a favorite kayaking destination. The camping area is situated above a high shoreline bank composed of glacial outwash. Apart from this primitive campground and a connecting trail from the parking area at the end of the road, little of this park has been impacted by public use. At low tide there is more than one-half mile of waterfront (including many tidepools) to explore.

*View from Obstruction Point (Entrance Mountain in the background)*

Inland towards the top of the hill, especially on its southern slopes, the forest (40 to 60% closed canopy) opens up considerably into a series of grass and moss-covered balds. Besides great cushions of moss and other bryophytes, you will also find Alaska oniongrass (*Melica subulata*), fragrant smelling yerba buena (*Satureja douglasii*), and broad-leaved stonecrop growing here.

The primary forest in this drier zone consists of mature Douglas fir mixed with shore pines. Throughout the area are numerous standing snags, and scattered wind-felled timber and large tree branches. Douglas squirrels are common here, their presence indicated by the scattered piles of fir cone scales which they leave behind in their quest for the seeds contained in the cones. This is also excellent habitat for the rarely seen northern flying squirrel. While Douglas squirrels are active during daylight hours, flying squirrels are strictly nocturnal. Every once in a while we glimpse one at dusk, gliding from tree to tree with apparent ease.

Other wildlife frequently observed in the park include black-tailed deer, river otters, rose-breasted nuthatches, pileated woodpeckers, dark-eyed juncos, and belted kingfishers.

*Indian pipe* (Monotropa uniflora) *growing through the duff on the forest floor*

# 34. Turtleback Mountain Preserve

**Size and Ownership:** 1,575 acres (San Juan County Land Bank.)

**Facilities:** Trails and dirt road tracks. [No vehicles, including bicycles. No fires, camping, or drinking water.] Dogs must be kept on leashes.

**Access:** From the Orcas Island ferry dock travel north on the Horseshoe Highway, turning left after 2.5 miles onto Deer Harbor Road. At the junction where Crow Valley Road begins (0.9 miles) you have a choice, as there are two entries (the North Entrance and the South Entrance) onto the preserve. To access the North Entrance turn right onto Crow Valley Road. Travel along this road for 2.7 miles; you will find the entrance to the preserve off to the left. To use the South Entrance, continue traveling west along Deer Harbor Road turning right onto Wild Rose Lane. (This is 2.2 miles from the Horseshoe Highway.) A welcome sign and a small parking area for cars are located at both entrances. The preserve is walk-in only.

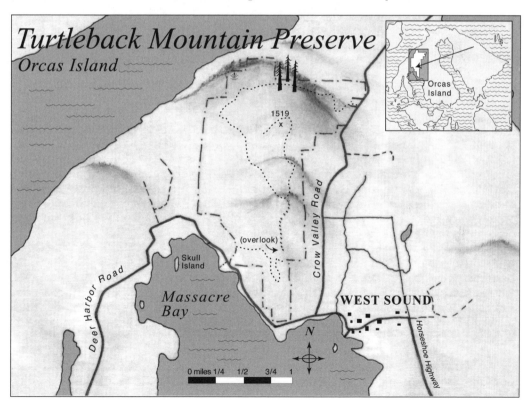

*The turtle-shaped profile of Turtleback Mountain as seen from San Juan Island*

At 1,519 feet above sea level, **Turtleback Mountain** is the second highest spot on Orcas Island. A distinctive landmark familiar to many residents of the San Juans, it has only recently been opened to public access. Following an intense fundraising campaign, the San Juan County Landbank acquired the mountain in November 2006. Additionally, to ensure continued public access and protection from development, the San Juan Preservation Trust holds a conservation easement for the entire preserve. A network of old logging roads and a connecting ridge-top trail currently provide walk-in only access to the preserve.

Turtleback Mountain is underlain by a mass of igneous rock. Much of this bedrock consists of *gabbro*, a type of lava that slowly cooled several miles beneath the sea floor and then later was thrust upward. Here and there can be seen dikes (intrusions) of a variety of granite called *tonalite*. Radiometric dating of both these minerals have yielded ages between 500 to 550 million years. This apparently makes them the oldest known rocks in the state of Washington.

Grassy rocky balds and savannah-like Garry oak woodlands occupy a large portion of the mountain's southern slopes. Patches of Pacific madrona and Rocky Mountain juniper can also be found in this region. The remainder of the mountain, including nearly all of its northern slope, is covered with coniferous forest dominated by Douglas fir. Western hemlock and western red cedar are also common here.

For many decades, the mountain was selectively logged. Much of its remaining forest is only 50 to 70 years old, but a few pockets of 200+ year-old timber still exist in some relatively inaccessible locations. Scattered all over the preserve are the rotting stumps (some with springboard notches dating from the early 1900s) of what used to be the area's primary forest.

The preserve also contains five scattered alder-fringed wetlands ranging from one half to nearly 4 acres in size. These wetlands occur around topographic depressions in the bedrock that are able to accumulate enough water during the rainy season to remain moist through the dry summer. Here on this well-drained mountain they provide crucial habitat for wildlife and certain moisture-loving plants. (There are no permanent streams in or near the preserve.)

*A view from the southern slopes of Turtleback Mountain Preserve. The rocky bald in the foreground supports remnant populations of several native prairie plant species.*

Wildlife species seen on Turtleback Mountain Preserve include golden eagle, bald eagle, merlin, osprey, Steller's jay, pileated woodpecker, marbled murrelet, black-tailed deer and Douglas squirrel.

# Part 5: THE LITTLE ISLANDS

*This classification includes islands that are less than twenty acres in size. Of the 6 sites described in this section just one is inhabited by humans. Camping is allowed on only two of the islands: Strawberry and Saddlebag (managed by the Dept. of Natural Resources and Washington State Parks respectively). Check on-site for camping fees and registration. None of these islands are accessible by public transportation and can only be approached by private boat or kayak.*

## 35. Yellow Island

**Size and Ownership:** Approximately 11.5 acres. (The Nature Conservancy.)

**Facilities:** Trails. [No camping, no toilets, no drinking water.] No pets allowed.

**Access:** *By boat:* Located in the western part of the Wasp Islands group, Yellow Island is 3.4 nautical miles northwest of the town of Friday Harbor (as the crow flies). There is a landing beach for dinghies and kayaks on the island's southern shore.

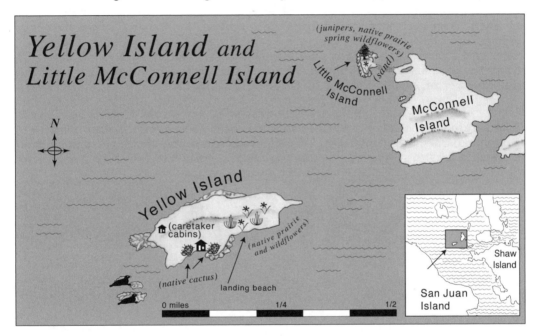

## 36. Little McConnell Island

**Size and Ownership:** Approximately 1.5 acres. (Federal land managed by the BLM.)

**Facilities:** None. [No camping, no toilets, no drinking water.]

**Access:** *By boat:* Located 0.4 mile northeast of Yellow Island in the Wasp Island group. There is a good landing beach for dinghies and kayaks on the north side of the small sand spit that connects larger McConnell Island to Little McConnell Island.

111

**Yellow Island** was purchased in 1980 by The Nature Conservancy to protect and enhance the island's native prairie and its amazing display of spring wildflowers. Each year, from late March until early June, the open grasslands occupying the island's eastern half and a smaller area in the northwest quarter become a cacophony of color. As the spring season progresses, brilliant colors emerge, come to dominance, and then recede as different species of wildflowers come into bloom.

The display generally begins with the yellow of the early buttercups, which are highlighted with splashes of white from the delicate fawn lilies. Next come the brown and green chocolate lilies, pink shooting stars, and bright red Indian paintbrushes. Then, sometime in mid-April, the spectacle climaxes in a virtual riot of red, yellow, and blues when the purple-blue camas blossoms finally open. The peak of the island's bloom period lasts only a few days (a week or so at most) before the flowers mature and begin to wither. Slowly the landscape reverts back to its normal dull-green color; by mid-June the flower show is all but over.

Although all the species of wildflowers that occur on Yellow Island can also be found in other parts of the San Juan Islands, nowhere in the region do they bloom over a large expanse in such intensity. Two important factors are key to maintaining these incredible floral displays: Firstly, there are no big herbivores (such as deer) to crop

*Spectacular spring wildflower display on Yellow Island*

the tender shoots of these plants. (Where deer populations are high, wildflower growth is reduced.) Secondly, the grassland must be periodically burned to retard overgrowth by woody shrubs and trees. Prairie grasses and wildflowers are adapted for periodic wildfire and often proliferate after a recent burn. The ecological stewards of Yellow Island Preserve generally try to do a controlled burn of these prairies about once every three years.

The Nature Conservancy welcomes visitors to Yellow Island Preserve but the island is small and can be easily damaged by careless visitors. Because of the prairie's fragile nature, they request that you remain on marked trails and comply with all other regulations. Soon after landing on the beach you will usually be greeted by one of the island's caretakers. Use of the preserve is restricted to the hours between sunrise and sunset. No picnicking, camping, or overnight moorage. Groups over six in number must have prior permission. Call: (206) 343-4344.

Nearby **Little McConnell Island** was named after Victor McConnell who maintained an orchard on adjacent McConnell Island in the late 1800s. Later, during the last quarter of the 20th Century, the smaller island was designated a state park.

*A tree leans out over the beach at Little McConnell Island*

However, when the State's parks commission decided not to renew its contract, the responsibility of stewardship was transferred to the BLM (Bureau of Land Management). Today, the island is a popular kayaking rest-stop and a "holding area" for folks waiting for their turn to walk among the spring wildflowers on nearby Yellow Island. (The Nature Conservancy limits the number of visitors allowed on Yellow Island at any given time.)

Although Little McConnell Island measures less than two acres in size, it offers more than a thousand feet of rocky waterfront to the casual shoreline explorer. During periods of low tide there are several shallow tide pools to poke around in.

The island itself is vegetated by a mixture of Rocky Mountain juniper, the odd Douglas fir or willow, and an important remnant of lowland Puget Prairie. Although it is not as spectacular as Yellow Island's wildflower display, Little McConnell Island's blossom-show can be quite pleasing. This small island supports a good mix of native grasses and forbs including camas, chocolate lily, Hooker's onion, and the cream-colored death camas.

Wildlife seen on the island include the occasional Columbian black-tailed deer, river otters, wild mink, white-crowned sparrows, northwest crows, and western tanagers.

# 37. Gossip Island

**Size and Ownership:** 2+ acres (State Land managed by Washington State Parks.)

**Facilities:** None. [No camping or drinking water.] No pets. Day use only.

**Access:** *By boat:* Located 3.25 nautical miles northwest of Roche Harbor (San Juan Island), Gossip Island sits at the mouth of Reid Harbor, a severe indentation in the eastern shoreline of Stuart Island. On Gossip Island's northern shore is a small snow-white beach composed of crushed shell that is excellent for landing kayaks and other small craft.

**Gossip Island** is a small undeveloped marine state park that has been maintained as a natural area due to its fragile Puget Prairie ecosystem and for the presence of a large colony of narrow-leaved sedum (*Sedum lanceolatum*), an endemic of the northern Puget Sound and Salish Sea region.

The island is open for day use only. Camping and campfires are strictly prohibited and the area is regularly patrolled by State Parks vessels and watchful residents on nearby Stuart Island.

After landing on the glaringly-white shell beach located on the island's north end, walk around to the right to hike along the rocky shoreline. (The beach is comprised mostly of crushed barnacle shells.) At the island's southern end, a short trail leads inland through a small prairie. Please be careful to stay on established pathways in order to avoid stepping on the many sedums which grow on the exposed bedrock. For much of the year these sedums are a barely-noticeable nondescript growth of greenish-gray. But in June and early July they sport masses of blazing yellow blossoms. At this time the rock faces seem to come alive with color.

Other interesting native plants found on the island include three species of ground orchid, purple camas, chocolate lilies, Puget Sound gumweed, and a few scraggly Rocky Mountain juniper trees. Occasionally, the lovely purple blossoms of the naked broomrape (*Orobanche uniflora*) appear. This parasite of sedums bears no leaves or stems and holds its upright one-inch tall flower just above ground level.

In the middle of the island sits a large granite boulder that was placed there by a receding glacier during the last ice age. Growing near this boulder is another artifact, a colony of domestic iris. This is the enduring legacy of a forgotten fisherman's wife who maintained a cabin on the island many years ago.

*Twisted old Rocky Mountain juniper and granite boulder on Gossip Island*

# 38. The Cone Islands

**Size and Ownership:** 9.85 acres (State Land managed by Washington State Parks.)

**Facilities:** None. [No camping or drinking water.] No pets.

**Access:** *By boat:* The Cone Islands are located 5.25 nautical miles due north of the San Juan Islands/Anacortes ferry dock near Shannon Point. There is a small beach situated on the northwest shore of Cone #1 that is suitable for landing kayaks and dinghies at low tide. All of the other islands in the Cone Island group have steep rocky shores and are not recommended for landing water craft or for "on-foot" exploration.

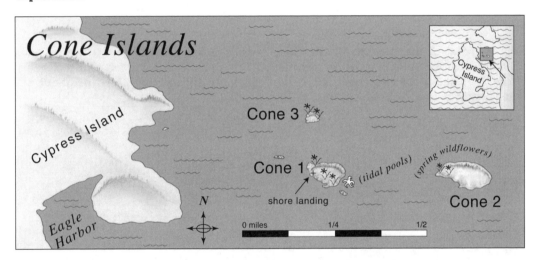

The Cone Islands are a picturesque group of three small rugged islands and several associated rocks situated at the north end of Bellingham Channel, about one-half mile offshore from northeastern Cypress Island. In 1973 the Federal Government deeded these islands to the State of Washington for use as a marine park. Fortunately, they have remained completely undeveloped and are still in their natural state.

Perhaps the best way to appreciate the Cone Islands is by paddling around them in a canoe or kayak. Their geographical location generally protects them from the strong winds that occasionally affect this region, particularly in nearby Rosario Strait. (Incidentally, the nearest public camping area is located at Pelican Beach on Cypress Island, a bit over a mile northwest of the Cone Islands.)

The smallest island in the group (Cone #3) protrudes barely 50 feet above sea level, while the largest (Cone #2) towers more than 106 feet above the visitor's head. Almost all of the shorelines of these islands are quite rocky and their upland slopes, very steep and uninviting. There is, however, a tiny low-tide landing beach located in a small cove on the northwest end of Cone #1. Although there are no trails leading into the island's precipitous interior, during April and early May numerous ranks of spring wildflowers can be admired close-up from the rocks surrounding the little cove.

During periods of high tide many of the Cone Islands' spring wildflower displays can actually be enjoyed from a small boat traveling close to shore. Some of the flowers that you may expect to see include miner's lettuce, large-flowered blue-eyed Mary, camas, chocolate lily, and least two varieties of Indian paintbrush. (Since the islands are so small in size, contain such rough terrain, and have no year-round source of freshwater, there are no resident deer to gobble up these lovely plants.)

Most of the tree cover on these islands is comprised of just two species: Pacific madrona and Douglas fir. As many of these trees are stunted and misshapen from their harsh growing conditions, there does not appear to be any indication that the islands have ever been commercially logged.

*A summer fog creeps in around Cone Island #3*

118

# 39. Strawberry Island

**Size and Ownership:** ± 11.5 acres (State Land managed by Washington State Department of Natural Resources.)

**Facilities:** Trails, picnic tables, and toilets. [No drinking water] Camping permitted. Pets must be kept on leashes.

**Access:** *By boat:* Strawberry Island lies off the west side of Cypress Island, 4 miles northwest of the San Juan Islands/Anacortes ferry dock. There is a rocky low-tide landing spot for kayaks and dinghies located in a small indentation on the southeast end of the island. (It can be rough during windy weather.)

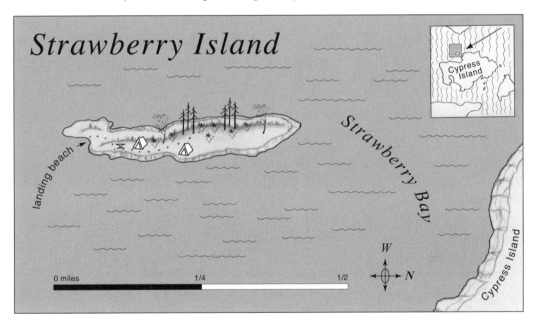

A third-of-a-mile long, north-to-south aligned ridge of rock, **Strawberry Island** receives few visitors outside of the short summer camping season. Due to an often difficult landing, the island's small campground is seldom full even during the peak of summer. The rewards are great, however, for anyone willing to make the extra effort.

This rocky island is covered with many pockets of soil and during April through May, it becomes ablaze with patches of bright wildflowers that grow in the open meadow-like areas. Buttercups, paintbrush, chocolate lily, camas, and (of course) strawberries are the main attractions but there is a native bush that also contributes its soft white orange-blossom-like flowers to the scene. This is the western serviceberry (*Amelanchier alnifolia*), a common edge-of-the-woods understory shrub found in the very driest areas of the San Juan archipelago (and in eastern Washington). In midsummer and early fall, serviceberries offer their pasty dark-colored fruits to passing birds and the occasional hiker. (Even though they are edible, they are an "acquired" taste for any would-be live-off-the-land type.)

The island's forest cover consists primarily of Douglas fir, Pacific madrona, and the occasional Rocky Mountain juniper or willow. While much of the shoreline is inaccessible from land, owing to its steepness, there is a trail that runs the length of the island through the forest along its central ridge. The highest spot along this trail is 125 feet above sea-level.

Although deer rarely swim out to Strawberry Island (believe me, they can easily do it!), it is most often frequented by river otters, the odd wild mink, and flocks of migrating songbirds in season. Except for brief periods in summer and the distant rumble of passing ships, this island remains a rare natural sanctuary of quietude.

*The west side of Strawberry Island seen from the northwest*

# 40. Saddlebag Island

**Size and Ownership:** ± 23 acres  (State Land managed by Washington State Parks.)

**Facilities:** Trails, picnic tables, and toilet. [No drinking water.] Camping allowed. Pets must be kept on leashes.

**Access:** *By boat:* Saddlebag Island is located 2 nautical miles northeast of the breakwater at the mouth of Cap Sante Marina in Anacortes. There is a good landing beach for kayaks and other small craft on the north shore of the island. Should the wind create rough seas from the North, there is also an acceptable landing beach on the island's southern shore. However, it is a rather steep climb to the top of the bluff above the beach here... especially if you are carrying heavy camping gear.

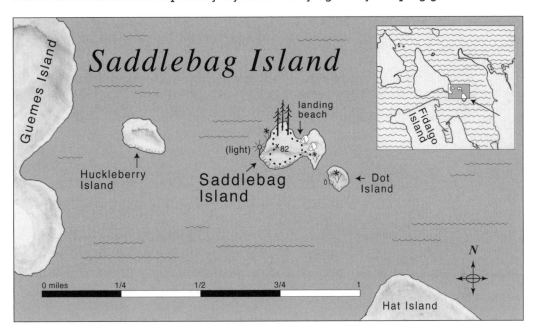

Saddlebag Island may have derived its name from it shape; the two unequal lobes connected by a broad strap of land does resemble a saddlebag, sort of. I'm assuming this, of course, since the actual reference seems to be lost to history. In 1841 the Wilkes expedition identified this island as one of the "Porpoise Rocks" but along with other changes over time, it got renamed. There is a concrete foundation located on the western end of the island that is probably the remains of an old dwelling. The island was designated a park after the State purchased it in 1974.

Much of Saddlebag Island's plant community is typical of the well-drained thin-soiled rocky islands found throughout our region. The primary forest cover consists mainly of Douglas fir mixed with broad-leafed maple, Douglas maple, Pacific madrona, Rocky Mountain juniper and bitter cherry. Several fine specimens of Pacific yew (*Taxus brevifolia*) can be seen along the well-worn trail that crosses the island from bay to bay. The head of the north bay has moist ground that supports Scouler's willow and cow parsnip. Nootka rose, snowberry, ocean spray, thimble-berry, tall Oregon grape and salal are typical of the shrub/scrub layer found on the island.

Along the island's southern flanks, between the ragged tree line and the rocky bluff of the shoreline, are a series of grassy balds that support a very different plant community. Here can be found remnant communities of native grassland that includes fescues, camas, death camas, showy chickweed, buttercups, sedum, chocolate lily, naked desert parsley, and star-flowered Solomon's seal (*Smilacina stellata*). Wildflower viewing is a popular attraction of the island when the flowers are in bloom from April through early June.

Wildlife seen on the island include the occasional black-tailed deer, voles, river otter, crows, winter wrens, savannah sparrows, fox sparrows, chickadees, great blue herons, belted kingfishers, northern flickers, and pileated woodpeckers.

*View from south side of Saddlebag Island*

# Part 6: THE OUTER ISLANDS

The 10 sites described in this section are located on islands that are larger than 50 acres in size. Indeed, several of these islands are more than 1,000 acres in extent and support small human settlements (with no visitor facilities). Also, a few isolated islands that were formerly occupied by 19th Century pioneer homesteads have since become state parks. None of these islands, however, are served by the Washington State Ferry System and are only accessible by chartering a boat or airplane (several of these islands have grass runways) or by private boat or kayak. Seven of these sites, which are managed by either the Department of Natural Resources or Washington State Parks, allow overnight camping. Check on-site for camping fees and registration.

## 41. Mary Leach Natural Area

**Size and Ownership:** 35 acres  (State Land managed by Washington Department of Fish and Wildlife.)

**Facilities:** Trails.  [No camping or drinking water.]  Dogs must be on leash.

**Access:** *By boat:* A somewhat obscure spot, the Mary Leach Natural Area is located in a bight on the southeastern shore of Sinclair Island about 6.5 miles north of the San Juan Islands/Anacortes ferry dock.  (GPS coordinates on the beach are 48.36.52° N and 122.39.45° W.)  The bottom rises gently here and the coarse gravel and cobble beach is adequate for landing kayaks and dinghies.  There is usually good anchorage nearby offshore for larger boats.

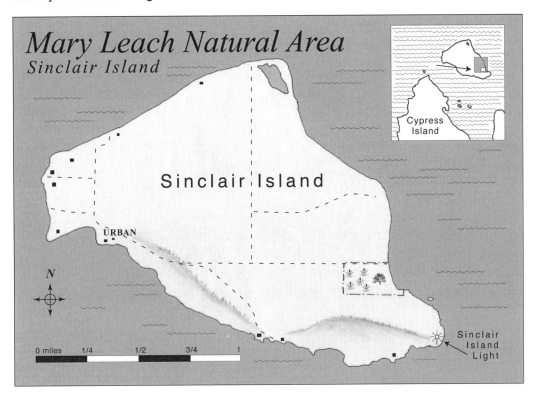

In 1974 Mary March Leach donated this 35 acre property, where she had spent much of her life, to the Washington Department of Game (now WDFW) to be preserved "in perpetuity" as a natural wildlife area.  The Department of Game agreed to manage the land for the enhancement of non-game wildlife and for public use.  During the following years the property has (fortunately) been mostly forgotten and natural succession is slowly changing the land back to its primeval state. It is an excellent example of what happens when a farm is abandoned to nature. The beauty of this site is that under continuing state protection the process of regeneration will not be interrupted by some new housing estate or commercial logging operation.

This land has endured many years of human use, as the overgrown welcome sign that still stands near Mary's old cabin attests: "The first post office on Sinclair Island was established here in 1894. Oxen were used to clear the land, where, in the early 1900s, cattle, sheep, poultry, orchards and gardens flourished. Logs were rafted in this bay for towing to the mill. Having provided shelter and a livelihood for the early settlers, it is fitting that the land be returned to nature."

But even after having donated this land to posterity, Mary Leach still worried about its future. In her 1988 book, <u>Cottonwood Collections (A History of Sinclair Island)</u>, she touchingly wrote:

> *"The forest primeval is gone, and a long period of time will pass before it is determined which species of plant life will prevail. Will it be the spread of tenacious evergreen blackberries, or the expansion of alder trees, the buckbrush, or the bracken? The dead and fallen fruit trees will decay and be absorbed - a matter of how many years?*
>
> *At the one-hundred year mark, from the time... the ground first felt the impact of the settler's axe and plow, one can only speculate on what the next hundred years will bring. The age of modern technology being what it is, this tiny dot of land could reach complete obscurity, or it could become a beautiful and harmonious wildlife refuge that would perpetuate the gifts of Nature."*

If Mary were alive today she might be pleased to see that her orchard of cherry, apple, and pear trees still stands, however motley, continuing to bear fruit in season for passing wildlife. She would note just how much of the open pasture has been invaded by the evergreen forest... and how the Douglas firs and other native trees are now beginning to dominate the fringes of the orchard. But she might also be dismayed to see how much the English ivy has spread.

To get from the shoreline to the upland area, you will find a steep "scramble path" up the clay embankment. The last time I visited the site, there was a decrepit log ladder pegged into the ground to help ease the climb. (Be careful though, one of the rungs broke away as I stepped on it and I nearly tumbled back down to the beach.) Once on top, however, a substantial trail leads into the interior.

*Cobble beach fronting the Mary Leach Natural Area*

Another feature of this site is a 1.6 acre marsh located west of the orchard. Originally this wetland was drained by a creek that ran to the bay. During the time the land was being farmed, the stream was dammed to create a pond. Now abandoned, the pond has gradually evolved into a marshy wetland choked with cattails. The path to the pond also disappeared as alders, salmonberry bushes and native crabapple trees reclaimed the area. Eventually the deep forest will overtake this spot, creating a canopy of western red cedars and Sitka spruce. But as long as there is sufficient moisture, it will always remain a wetland.

Red huckleberry (*Vaccinium parviflorum*) and vine maple (*Acer circinatum*) are two native plants that are common on this part of Sinclair Island. These species are not generally found in the San Juan Islands. Wildlife you might encounter here include wild turkeys, great blue herons, river otter, bald eagles, belted kingfishers, cedar waxwings, red-tailed hawks, and barred owls.

# 42. Cypress Island Natural Area Preserve

**Size and Ownership:** ± 202.25 acres [Northern Unit] (State Land managed by Washington Department of Natural Resources.)

**Facilities:** Trails. Picnic tables and toilets at Pelican Beach. [No drinking water.] Camping at Pelican Beach Recreation Site. No dogs allowed.

**Access:** *By boat:* Pelican Beach is located on the northeast end of Cypress Island, slightly more than 6.25 nautical miles (as the crow flies) northwest of the San Juan Islands/Anacortes ferry dock. (The GPS coordinates for the beach are 48.36.13N and 122.42.15W.)

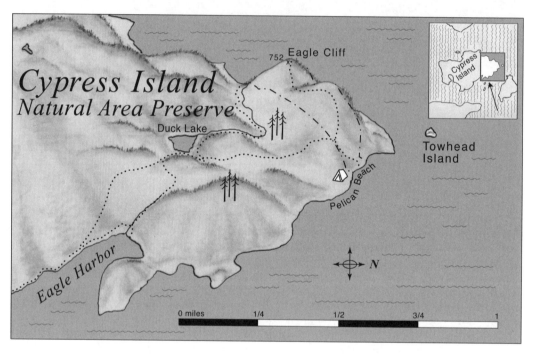

Except for a small scatter of buildings located at the head of Secret Harbor and along the shore of Strawberry Bay, most of **Cypress Island** has remained fairly undeveloped. The name "Cypress Island" is a bit of a misnomer bestowed in 1792 when a landing party from Capt. George Vancouver's ship mistook the island's abundant junipers for cypress trees. They were not entirely wrong, however, junipers actually *are* in the cypress family [*Cupressaceae*].) Today a large portion of this 5,500+ acre island is owned by the State and managed under two programs by the Washington Department of Natural Resources. More than 3,900 acres of the island's terrestrial habitat and public tidelands was designated in 1987 as a Natural Resource

Conservation Area (NRCA). Now the southern two-thirds of the island supports the only protected low-elevation forest growing on serpentine soils in Washington. (Please turn to pages 157-158 for a discussion about the effects that serpentine soils have on native plant communities.) For most visitors, however, this is essentially a limited public recreation area that allows no vehicle access and camping only in designated locations. Hikers are welcome, however, to explore the miles of trails and abandoned roads that often lead to scenic upland vistas or secluded shoreline coves. In 2007 the tidelands and all of the waters surrounding Cypress Island (including Strawberry Island and the Cone Islands) ranging from about 2,000 feet to more than a mile offshore were designated as the Cypress Island Aquatic Reserve.

An additional 1,073 acres of the island's uplands have been allocated into a Natural Area Preserve (NAP). With the intention of protecting unique or irreplaceable native plants and animals, NAPs normally have severely limited public access. Due to the sensitivity of these sites, most visits are restricted to educational field trips and approved scientific research. The Cypress Island NAP consists of two separate units.

Notwithstanding, the 200 plus acre northern section of the NAP is a notable exception to WDNR's exclusion policy for it provides a trail that invites public use. The trail begins near the information kiosk at Pelican Beach Campground and it breathtakingly terminates after about a mile atop 752 foot-high **Eagle Cliff**. This heart-pounding climb is well worth the effort; the view here is simply spectacular.

On the way to the summit of Eagle Cliff you may notice a rather unassuming shrub with leathery gray-green ovate leaves that bears dense clusters of red berries in summer. This is hairy manzanita (*Arctostaphylos columbiana*), a close relative of the Pacific madrona. It is an inhabitant of the open ridges of Cypress Island and is rarely found anywhere else in the San Juan Islands.

The trail to Eagle Cliff passes through a mixed coniferous successionary forest dominated by western red cedar and Douglas fir. The presence of spring-board notches in some of the old tree stumps indicate that the area was commercially logged early in the 20th Century. Other tree species present here include the broad-leaved maple, Douglas maple, choke cherry, red alder, grand fir and western hemlock (look for seedling hemlocks growing on prostrate nurse logs). Near the top of the trail the forest noticeably thins out, becoming more dominated by shore pines and Rocky Mountain juniper. Glacial striations can easily be seen on some of the rock-faces as you near the summit.

Cypress Island NAP also protects some outstanding examples of native fescue-dominated grassland and some special low elevation sphagnum bogs and freshwater wetlands.

*View across Haro Strait from near the top of Eagle Cliff*
*on Cypress Island*

One splendid wetland that you can easily visit is **Duck Lake**. (It's located outside of the NAP; just follow the mile-long trail south from Pelican Beach Campground.) The lake is almost completely covered with native yellow pond lily (*Nuphar luteum* ssp. *polysepalum*) with only small patches of open water showing here and there. Surrounded by a zone of standing snags and partly dead trees, this area is particularly good wildlife habitat. Besides pond lily, the lake contains a rich variety of aquatic plants including sedges, cattail, mare's-tail, pondweed, water smartweed, and bladderwort. The basin that contains Duck Lake, being surrounded by mountains, gives it the appearance of being much more remote than it really is. To the Northwest, between two of those hills, lies the intermittent watercourse that tentatively connects this lake to the sea.

A few of the bird species that I've observed in this region include osprey, bald eagle, brown tree creeper, marsh wren, rose-breasted nuthatch, barred owl, mountain chickadee, and large flocks of mallard ducks.

# 43. Jones Island

**Size and Ownership:** 186.75 acres (Federal Land managed by Washington State Parks.)

**Facilities:** Trails, dock, mooring buoys, picnic tables, drinking water (in spring and summer) and composting toilets. [Camping permitted.] Dogs must be kept on leash.

**Access:** *By boat:* Jones Island is located 0.4 miles off the southwestern end of Orcas Island, about 4.5 miles northwest of the town of Friday Harbor (as the crow flies). There are several gravelly beaches suitable for landing kayaks or dinghies and a boat dock located in the island's northern bay.

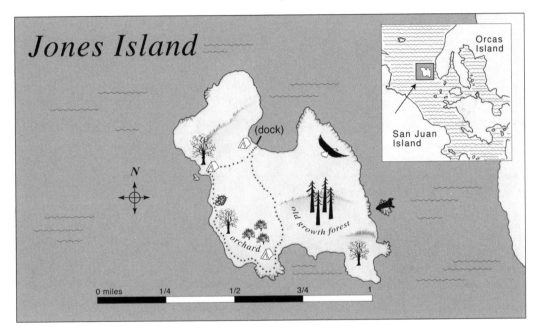

Administered as a Washington State Marine Park, **Jones Island** is a popular destination for all kinds of holiday boaters. The park boasts a small pier and three separate camping areas. One of these campgrounds is managed expressly for "human powered watercraft" (i.e. kayakers and canoeists) while another (the southern campground) can accommodate large groups. But even if the camping areas do get rather crowded now and then, it is still one of my favorite natural areas in the San Juans.

The island has over three miles of rocky shoreline interrupted only by the occasional scallop of a pebbly beach, particularly in the north and south. Several paths (including a couple of "unofficial" trails) allow hikers to explore nearly two-thirds of this rugged coastline.

Many years ago I saw my first orca (killer whale) in the wild from one of the island's trails. An entire family group of these giant dolphins was traveling just off-shore when suddenly one them vaulted out of the water below me. Seemingly in slow motion, it rose to the height of the bluff where I was sitting. For a moment or two our eyes met across the short expanse of air between us... then the huge animal fell back into the water with a tremendous splash and was gone. I have never felt quite the same about the world ever since.

*The rugged coast of Jones Island*

The island's rocky interior attains a maximum height of 206 feet above sea level on an evergreen-forested hillock located near its center. Connecting the north and south campgrounds, a 0.45 mile-long trail crosses the low saddle that separates the island's two principal hills. Broad-leaved maple, Douglas fir, hemlock, and red cedar are abundant here but it is not until you pass through the fruit orchard to reach the southern shoreline that the forest really changes substantially. (Incidentally, this orchard appears on an 1885 US Army map of the island and is a favorite summer hangout for many of the island's deer.)

Windswept in winter and spring, hot and dry in summer, the well-drained southern and western slopes of Jones Island supports a "fringe forest" of Pacific madrona, shore pines, Rocky Mountain junipers, and Garry oaks (*Quercus garryana*). Although a few of the oaks can be seen growing near the foreshore, a native plants survey revealed that hundreds more of these trees were "embedded" in the evergreen forest further inland. Natural succession aided by the exclusion of wildfire has allowed the firs to dominate and threaten the Garry oaks by overshadowing these ecologically important and increasingly rare hardwood trees. Much to its credit, the park's managers have formed a special team to try and conserve the oaks. (For more about Garry oak ecology please turn to pages 40-41.)

In the southwest part of the island you may notice the region's only species of native cactus growing along the shoreline trail. Actually, most people don't heed these low growing 1 to 2 square-foot patches of cryptically-colored spiny masses until they either painfully sit on them or they see them in bloom. The brittle cactus (*Opuntia fragilis*) displays 2-inch-diameter intensely yellow blossoms that make them stand out for a few short weeks in late June and early July. After the bloom period, they seem to disappear into the grass again.

Some of the wildlife that you are likely to see while exploring Jones Island include bald eagles (there is an active nest in the dense forest on the island), river otters, harbor seals on the rocks off the eastern side of the island, an occasional raccoon and, of course, the ubiquitous deer.

Deer are especially common around the camps where they have become so accustomed to people that visitors sometimes hand-feed them bits of bread or fists full of maple leaves (against park rules). "Officially" these are Columbian black-tailed deer but if you observe closely, you may occasionally see an individual adult or two that sports a spotted belly. These are actually exotic fallow deer *(Dama dama)*. How did they get on Jones Island? Simple! They swam. I've observed deer swimming more than a mile offshore and many local folks know that there are *plenty* of fallow deer living on nearby Spieden Island. I've also examined documents that indicate during the 1920s and early 30s there were at least two introductions of fallow deer onto Orcas Island by Robert Moran, the founder of Rosario Resort. And I have a copy of a letter written to the local Game Commission dated around that time which decries the "inbred" and "puny" qualities of our local deer population and urges stocking the islands with more "robust" varieties for hunting purposes. Apparently the letter-writer's proposition was successful.

## 44. James Island

**Size and Ownership:** 116.5 acres (State Land managed by Washington State Parks.)

**Facilities:** Trails, boat dock, picnic tables, campsites, and toilets. [No drinking water.] Dogs must be kept on leash.

**Access:** *By boat:* James Island is located just south of the east entrance to Thatcher Pass, about 0.25 miles east of Decatur Head on the east coast of Decatur Island. It is 3.2 nautical miles westward across Rosario Strait from the Washington Park public boat ramp near Anacortes. There is a small pier and float located on the western side of the island and (depending on the state of the wind and tide) two gravelly beaches on the island's eastern side that are suitable for landing kayaks or dinghies.

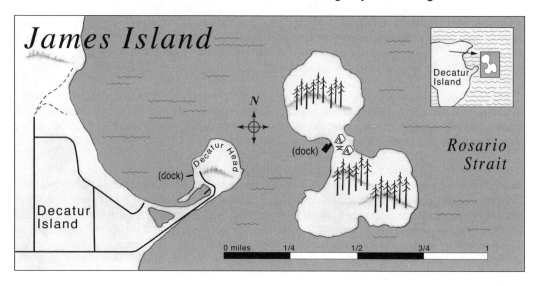

Shaped a bit like a smashed weightlifter's dumbbell, **James Island** has long been administered as a Washington State Marine Park. Barely three-quarters of a mile in length, the island essentially consists of two hilly lobes connected by a low neck of land. At 274 feet above mean sea level, the northern hill is the island's highest point. Almost all of the developed facilities on the island are located on the stretch of lowland that connects the two hilly lobes.

Outside of the camping and picnic areas, most of the island consists of quite rugged terrain. Trails leading uphill quickly peter out to become ill-defined paths, and there are only a few places along the rocky coast (apart from that convenient neck of land) where a boat can be safely landed. This ruggedness is at once this island natural area's beauty and part of its protection; both of those hilly lobes support patches of mature evergreen forest that appear to have been spared the woodsman's axe because of the rough topography. Dominated by Douglas fir, a few of these forest trees have become quite large.

The thin, well drained soils that cap the bedrock make this a very dry forest for much of the year (when it's not actually raining). Consequently, the mossy forest-floor on these hilly slopes supports very little underbrush. On a few of the southern exposures, particularly above the south end of the island, the forest gives way to open grassy areas that support a modest wildflower show in spring.

Wildlife seen on and around James Island include bald eagles, great horned owls, black turnstones, great blue herons, double-crested cormorants, pigeon guillemots (nesting on rocky cliffs above the water), river otter, and the occasional black-tailed deer. (During one recent visit to the island we marveled as we watched a pair of deer swim out from Decatur Head and then haul themselves up the steep slopes of James Island's northern hill.) In the past, food-filching raccoons have been a nuisance for overnight campers.

*The steep shoreline of James Island (Decatur Island is in the background)*

# 45. Clark Island

**Size and Ownership:** ± 55 acres (State Land managed by Washington State Parks.)

**Facilities:** Trails, picnic tables, campsites, and toilets. [No drinking water.] Dogs must be kept on leash.

**Access:** *By boat:* Clark Island is located 2.25 nautical miles northwest of Lawrence Point on the northeastern tip of Orcas Island. Additionally, it is 10.5 miles west (as the crow flies) of the Fairhaven Boat Ramp in Bellingham. There are excellent beaches suitable for landing kayaks and dinghies located on either side of the island.

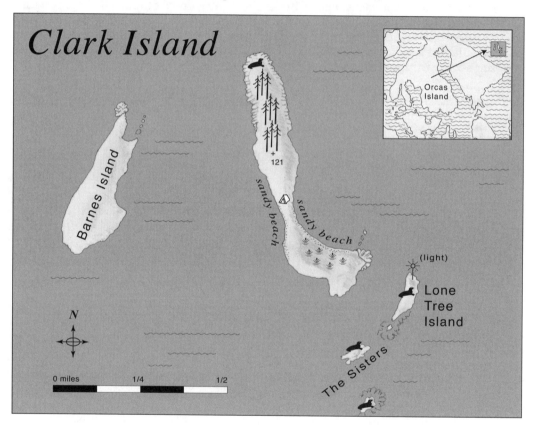

    **Clark Island** seems to be one of the lesser-visited State Marine Parks in the San Juan Islands. One reason for this might be that it is rather isolated, with few amenities. Also, because of the rugged steep-sided terrain of this narrow mile-long island, there are few places to walk other than along its beaches or one of the short tracks that cross its narrow waist near the camping area and toilets.

The north and south sections of this island are characterized by rocky outcrops sprinkled with pockets of glacial till. Most of the bedrock consists of sedimentary conglomerates. The island's protected western beach seems to be composed primarily of fine sand, while the beach on the more exposed eastern side is decidedly pebbly.

Its Douglas fir-dominated forest is interspersed with Douglas maple, Pacific yew, Pacific madrona, grand fir, shore pine, and willow. (Up on the ridge towards the north end is a nearly pure stand of graceful madronas.) This large variety of tree (big for the size of the area they occupy) is probably the beneficial result of past wildfires. Indeed, some older Douglas fir trunks bear fire scars that reach 20 to 30 feet up from the ground. The shrubbery understory is also varied and includes wild rose, snowberry, ocean spray, red huckleberry, and western serviceberry.

The island's most significant upland ecological feature, however, is a small sensitive wetland located just above the eastern beach. Its deep saturated soils are almost completely organic, indicating that it has occupied this site for many hundreds of years. A few of its indicator plants include soft rush, water parsley, poison hemlock, beach grass, hardhack, twinberry, and a nice patch of Pacific cinquefoil.

*Southeast Clark Island*

137

# 46. Matia Island

**Size and Ownership:** 154.4 acres (Federal Land managed by Washington State Parks and U.S. Fish and Wildlife.)

**Facilities:** Boat dock, trails, picnic tables, campsites, and toilets. [No drinking water.] Dogs must be kept on leash on dock and in camp. No pets on loop trail.

**Access:** *By boat:* The Matia Island dock located in Rolfe Cove is 4.75 nautical miles northeast of Point Doughty (as the crow flies) on the northwestern tip of Orcas Island. From the mainland, the Matia Island dock is 6 miles southwest of the marina at Sandy Point just west of the city of Bellingham.

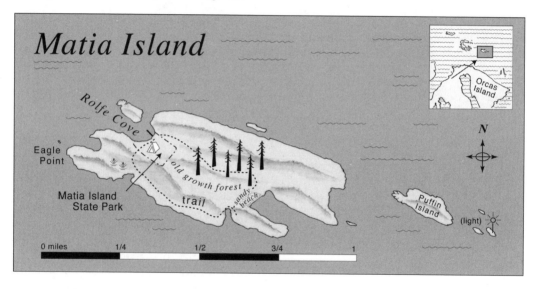

Federally owned **Matia Island** is designated as a National Wildlife Refuge, part of the San Juan Islands National Wildlife Refuge system. A small portion of the island, totaling about 5 acres, is currently managed as a State Marine Park offering limited camping facilities. On the southeast end of the island stand a few scraggly fruit trees, remnants of an old homestead. A fox farm is said to have been operated here in the 1920s.

Like many of the northern San Juans, Matia Island's bedrock is primarily sandstone, often filled with a conglomerate of water-worn rocks and pebbles. Around the entrance to Rolfe Cove, especially on the little unnamed island in front of the dock, are many gargoyle-like weathered sandstone shapes. I dubbed a stern-looking one on its east shore the "mother-in-law rock." Nearby, on the western tip of Matia Island at Eagle Point, is an excellent example of how this sandstone, originally formed in crossbedded horizontal layers, has been tilted nearly vertical by geologic forces. (For a further discussion about the geology of this region, turn to pages 142-143 which describes the geology of neighboring Sucia Island.)

A mile-long loop trail, beginning and ending near the head of the dock, offers limited access to the island's interior. Along the northern section of its loop, the trail passes through an area of old growth forest. Springboard notches in many of the stumps indicate that the area was logged in the days of the crosscut hand-saw sometime during the early 20th Century. The island was "high-graded" to extract only the most valuable timber because all of the stumps are western red cedar.

The forest here is still impressive, however. There are ranks of tall noble fir, broadleaf maple, red cedar, and some big Douglas firs more than five feet in diameter (dbh). In some places the canopy closure is more than eighty percent, allowing some fine patches of sword fern (*Polystichum munitum*) to grow in the darkened understory. A few older trees bear fire scars more than 30 feet up their trunks, historical evidence of past wildfires. One large trailside red cedar (which for

*Rolfe Cove from Matia Island*

139

some reason was spared the woodsman's saw) has a hollow in its trunk big enough to shelter at least three people.

At the eastern end of the island, the loop trail skirts a lovely rectangular-shaped shallow bay before turning westward to parallel the southern coast. It's well worth a pause on its small beach before heading on down the trail. In spring you can often see pigeon guillemots (a black and white pigeon-shaped seabird with bright red feet) flying to and from their nests on the rocky cliffs lining the north side of the bay. Watch also for bald eagles perched on exposed trees and black oystercatchers (with their red-orange feet and beaks) on the rocks near the water.

Near the western end of the island, just before it arrives back at its beginning, the loop trail passes a small forested wetland. Approximately 2 acres in size, this several-hundred-foot long narrow marsh drains into the small cove just north of Eagle Point. Bordered by red alder and Sitka spruce, it is filled with slough sedge (*Carex obnupta*), water parsley, a bit of deadly poisonous water hemlock, and lots of cattails. This wetland is an important year-round freshwater source for local wildlife.

*Shallow bay on east end of Matia Island*

# 47. Sucia Island

**Size and Ownership:** 564 acres [not including 63 acres of private property located on Justice, North Finger and South Finger islands.]  (The remainder is State Land managed by Washington State Parks.)

**Facilities:**  Boat dock, trails, picnic tables, campsites, drinking water, and toilets. Dogs must be kept on leash.

**Access:**  *By boat:* The public docks in Fossil Bay are located 3.1 nautical miles northeast (as the crow flies) from Point Doughty on northwestern Orcas Island.

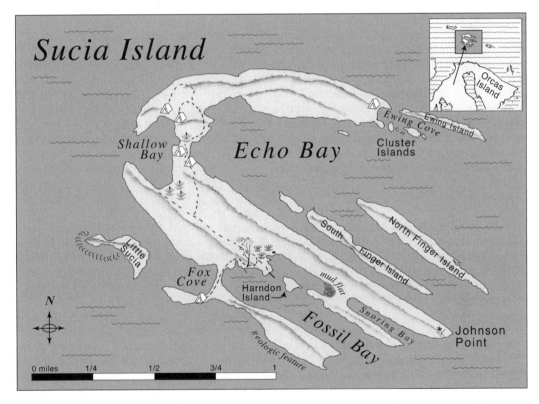

Shaped somewhat like a skeletal hand, **Sucia Island** is not just a single land-mass but a closely related group of 13 separate islands: Sucia, Little Sucia, Harndon, South Finger, North Finger, Justice, Ewing, the five Cluster Islands, and an unnamed island in Echo Bay.  All of the islands except North Finger, South Finger, and the upper half of Justice (so named after the property was confiscated from a convicted drug dealer) are managed collectively as the Sucia Island Marine State Park.

In 1959 almost half of the Sucia Island group was purchased by the Puget Sound Interclub Association and placed in the trust of the State for "Yachtsmen forever." Much to everyone's benefit, "yachty" and landlubber alike, it and an adjacent state-owned property were soon declared a State Park. All told, this popular destination offers more than 14.5 miles of shoreline for exploration. It is estimated that nearly 100,000 people use its extensive boating and camping amenities each year.

At first glance, this lovely island seems at odds with its name. In Spanish, "sucia" means "dirty" or "foul" in the nautical sense. Apparently the 1791 explorers from Spain felt that the sea-bottom around this group of islands was far too cluttered and "reefy" to offer clean anchorage for one of their ungainly ships.

But it is this very "reefyness," resulting from an interesting geological history, that gives the area its unique character. The bedrock of these islands consists of sandstones, shales, and gravelly conglomerates, all thought to be between 45 and 80 million years old. During that time long ago, a broad estuary apparently dominated this region. Across its wide flood-plain grew clumps of palmetto and other tropical plants. Sea animals such as clams (*Inoceramus sp.*), snails, and ammonites (an extinct relative of the chambered nautilus), lived and died in its waters and were buried in its sediments. Occasionally the rivers that mouthed into this estuary flooded and the fine estuarine sediments containing the shells were covered with layers of sand. Really big floods brought gravel from upstream, spreading it across a growing underwater delta.

Over time and from the pressure from being deeply buried, these layers slowly hardened and became sandstone, mudstone, and other sedimentary rock. One striking feature of these rocks, which provides a clue to their origin, is their cross-bedding. This occurs when a river fills its bed with sediment, causing the stream to change its direction of flow. The sediments are aligned in the direction of the flow of the water as they are deposited and when the stream changes direction, the angle of the next layer of sediment (the bedding) also changes.

As more time passed, the trapped shells became fossils. Geologic forces cracked, folded, and tilted those beds of sandstone and shale from a horizontal plane to almost vertical. Some of it was pushed up to the earth's surface. Vast ice sheets, some more than 5,000 feet thick, also came and went. They covered the region with pulverized rock and then with gravelly outwash when the ice finally melted. Large parts of the exposed bedrock resisted and remained in place.

Today, erosion has revealed long parallel ridges of tilted sandstone. In some locations shallow bays have formed between these ridges. In other places, the stone has been eroded into curious shapes like that of Mushroom Rock in Fox Cove or into fantastic patterns reminiscent of a honeybee's comb. (This pattern is called honey-comb weathering, a product of the "splash zone" in this coastal area. When the seawater sloshed onto the rock evaporates, salt crystals form and dislodge a few grains of sand, creating a tiny pit. Over a span of many years the pits slowly enlarge and coalesce with one other as the softer stone is removed. [See photo on page 90.] An alternate explanation for this effect holds that moisture gathering in the hollows, "draws" soluble salts out of the rock and carries it to the surface, where salt crystals fret the grains away. Either way, the process creates some interesting rock-forms.)

Incidentally, the geologic folding of those ancient beds of shale and sandstone brought many interesting marine fossils to the surface, most of them shells. Some nice examples can be seen on the southeast arm of Sucia Island itself. (Be warned, however, that fossil collecting in the State Park is strictly prohibited.)

*Boulder-strewn beach on southern shore of Sucia Island*
*(Honeycomb weathering can be seen in the sandstone pavement on the left.)*

Located at the south end of Shallow Bay is a wedge-shaped open flat about five aces in extent. Fluctuating water levels in this ancient peat bog have drowned a grove of cedars, many of which are still standing. This is the more obvious part of a very significant wetland that lies in the forest between the two bracketing ridges on either side of the cedar grove. Long and narrow, this wetland extends 0.7 miles eastward all the way to Mud Bay. At a point not quite midway along its length, the flow direction of the surface and subsurface waters switches from westward to east.

One end of the wetland drains through the gravel beach-berm into Shallow Bay; the other end flows into Mud Bay via a small saltmarsh creek.

There is a trail running between Mud Bay and Shallow Bay that parallels this wetland. Beginning at the forest line on the Shallow Bay end is a large clone of quaking aspen (*Populus tremuloides*), an uncommon wetland tree species in the San Juan Islands. Most likely, this entire grove is composed of a single genetic individual, linked together by underground network of rhizomatous roots. Some of the largest living organisms ever recorded have been aspen groves.

I won't bother to present you with a catalogue of the plants found in this wetland but watch for changes in the wetland's character as you travel inland: cattails giving way to red osier dogwoods, willows replacing the dogwoods and then being replaced in turn by red cedar and thimbleberries. In less wetter areas grow grand firs; on still drier ground stand the Douglas firs.

As you approach Mud Bay, the order of transition becomes somewhat reversed. Back in the open, the emergent portion of this wetland is transformed into a small estuarine saltmarsh just before it drains into the bay, north of the public dock.

*Drowned cedar trees at the head of Shallow Bay*

144

# 48. Patos Island

**Size and Ownership:** 208.3 acres (Federal Land managed by the Bureau of Land Management with a cooperative agreement with the Washington State Parks Commission.)

**Facilities:** Trails, picnic tables, campsites, and toilets. [No drinking water.] Dogs must be kept on leash.

**Access:** *By boat:* The lighthouse at Alden Point is 3 nautical miles due east of East Point Lighthouse on Saturna Island (Canada) and 4.6 miles northwest of Point Doughty on Orcas Island (USA). There is a sandy beach suitable for landing small craft next to the camping area at the east end of Active Cove.

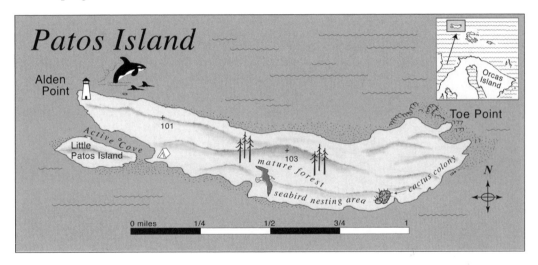

In 1792 Spanish explorers Galliano and Valdez named this island in the northern San Juan archipelago "Isla de Patos" (the Island of Ducks). **Patos Island** still has a lot of birds about it, including a seabird nesting area on the island's rocky southern cliffs. Along with several other species, pigeon guillemots are occasionally common there. Clumps of the rare brittle cactus (*Opuntia fragilis*) have also been spotted growing on some of the isolated rocky shelves of these inaccessible sandstone cliffs. Found on no other island in the San Juans, oak ferns (*Gymnocarpium dryopteris* var. *disjunctum*) grow in Pato's tall forest.

Historically, this island had been an important stopping-over place for certain Native Americans. They left behind numerous shell-middens around the island as evidence. By the late 1800s, however, the natives were long gone and Patos Island had been designated as a lighthouse reserve. A fox farm was established on the island in the 1920s but it only lasted for a few years. For the past thirty years or so after the Coast Guard automated the lighthouse, the island has been managed as a state marine park. (That lease with the federal government has since expired.) Patos Island is now under the stewardship of the U.S. Bureau of Land Management with a cooperative management agreement with Washington State Parks for continued maintenance of the camping area and to provide enforcement patrols.

Having a geology similar to that of the Sucia group, Patos Island is 1.5 miles in length (from the lighthouse at Alden Point to Toe Point on its eastern end). There used to be a 1.5-mile-long loop trail extending from the camping area but lately it seems neglected and its furthest reaches have become overgrown with salal and other shrubs. The interior of the island and its mature evergreen forest are becoming increasingly wild but portions of it can still be examined, especially near the campground. The best method of exploring the island is by water, preferably in a sea kayak or rowing dory. In April and May, spring wildflowers adorn some of the grassy balds that fringe stretches of this island's 3.75-mile-long coastline.

Offshore, in the deep waters just west of the lighthouse, large pods of orcas (killer whales) and harbor porpoises are often seen during late summer, feeding and surfacing around the swirling upwellings caused by strong tidal currents.

*Rocky shore at low tide on Patos Island*

## 49. Cowlitz Bay Preserve

**Size and Ownership:** 271.75 acres  (The Nature Conservancy.)

**Facilities:** Trail. [No drinking water or toilets.]  Camping and pets strictly prohibited.

**Access:** *By boat:* The beach landing site for Cowlitz Bay Preserve on Waldron Island is 9.6 nautical miles north-northwest of the marina in Friday Harbor and 6.6 miles northeast of the Roche Harbor marina (as the crow flies).  The sandy/pebbly beach here is shallow but sufficient for landing kayaks or dinghies.  Larger boats must be anchored offshore.  During periods of low tide, a large expanse of beach is exposed and you may have to slog up to the foreshore where the preserve trail begins.

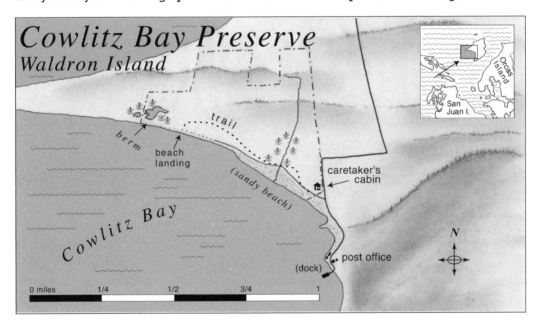

**Cowlitz Bay Preserve** is a splendid example of what happens when logged, cultivated, and grazed land is allowed to revert back to its natural state.  Located on the southern shores of Waldron Island, the property was cleared in the late 1800s and used for agriculture for nearly 75 years.  It was purchased by the Nature Conservancy and established as a preserve in 1968.

Since Waldron Island receives few visitors, it has remained a shyly quiet community that seems to hark back to a bygone age.  (There are no grocery stores, gas stations, restaurants, public telephones, or electrical service here.  If you want to chat with a local or mail a letter, however, there is a post office in an old log cabin located above the community dock.)

147

Wetlands are among the primary features in Cowlitz Bay Preserve. Located just west of where the preserve trail begins at the landing beach, there is an accretion shoreform enclosing a marsh with a small shallow lagoon. Many years ago (in the 1880s and early 1900s) the barrier berm fronting the lagoon had a low spot in it that allowed sea water to pour in during high tide. Over the intervening years the berm has gradually been built up higher with accumulations of sand and gravel and now even much of the lagoon has filled up with gritty mud. Although the lagoon still has elevated salinity levels, often ranging from 500 to 600 milligrams of salt per liter, it has essentially become a freshwater ecosystem. Almost all of the wetland plants growing around and in it, including cattail, soft-stemmed rush, Pacific cinquefoil, and exotic reed canarygrass, are generally considered to be freshwater indicators. However, its increased salinity is still reflected in the presence of Pacific silverweed (*Potentilla pacifica*), a plant often found on the fringes of salt marshes. The berm now appears to be expanding seaward.

*The beach at Cowlitz Bay Preserve*
*(looking west from the top of the bluff)*

Near the beginning of the trail you will encounter a large wooden sign announcing the preserve and some of its prohibitions (no smoking, for instance). From here the trail follows the crest of a long bluff, passing through a mixture of evergreen forest, woody scrub, and transitional grassland. Rising to over 60 feet high, the steep bluff is composed of a mixture of sandy clay and gravel and appears to be the eroded edge of a large glacial outwash deposit that fills the valley between the two low hills on the west and the high ridge to the east.

A large freshwater wetland more than 20 acres in size is perched on this glacial deposit. In times past while the land was being farmed, there was a serious effort to "reclaim" this wetland by draining it. Although the attempt was not totally successful, a large V-shaped notch in the bluff was created. (Recalling the use of cheap labor from new immigrants, this man-made outlet is locally referred to as "Chinaman's ditch.") Cutting into the face of the bluff nearly down to the level of the beach, it is a noticeable landmark when viewed from the bay.

In 1995 several beavers mysteriously arrived on the island and took up residence in the upper marsh. After eight years the beavers suddenly vanished, leaving behind a very much improved wetland system. (How the beavers originally got here and where they went has been a subject of much speculation.) This area is outstanding for its abundance of waterfowl and marsh birds.

There are no native grasses or forbs present in any of the grassland areas that remain in the preserve... except on the shoulder of the bluff. Here you can find red fescue, Puget Sound gumweed, great camas, fireweed, bi-colored lupine, and meadow lotus (*Lotus denticulatus*) among others. There are two likely reasons why these plants occur here but not out in the open meadows; both of them have to do with grazing animals. Firstly, there are no deer on Waldron Island. Many of these plants would have a hard time if deer were present because they like to eat them. The second reason is that when the property was being farmed, it had grazing livestock, such as sheep. The sheep lived in the pastures but did not heavily graze the shoulder of the bluff for fear of falling over the edge. The farmer may even have prevented the sheep from approaching the edge with a fence. Perhaps the unintended result from that concern was to create a linear refugia for native plants along the line of the bluff.

The trail eventually leads to the home of the preserve's longtime caretaker, Tony Scruton. This is a private residence. Likely as not, however, he'll be somewhere nearby unless he is busy bringing over the island's mail in his boat. Should you meet him, most likely he can answer any questions you may have about the preserve.

Before the trail reaches the caretaker's cabin, it passes through several large dense thickets of wild rose and snowberry (*Symphoricarpos albus*). This is part of the successionary scrub that is gradually replacing the open pasture land. Here and there, rank groves of wild cherry trees are beginning to dominate the scrub and eventually will help replace it. Spreading by means of horizontal root suckers, these trees are among the few species that can penetrate the rose thickets. Given time, however, the cherries themselves will give way to the firs and other species of the climax forest. In the meantime, the cherries are very likely an important seasonal food source for some of the area's bird species.

Squatting in the mowed lanes that thread through these dense thickets, you may see the occasional cottontail rabbit, an introduced species on the island. If you don't see the rabbits themselves, look for bits of hide and fur. That will be the spot where a hawk or an owl has made a kill. These trails have become favorite "killing alleys" for some of the local raptors.

Other wildlife commonly seen in the preserve are bald eagles, osprey, northwest crow, river otters, Canada geese, mallard ducks, tree swallows, marsh wrens, western tanagers, nuthatches, common yellowthroats, rufous-sided towhees, and red-winged blackbirds.

*Old wagon-wheel among the wildflowers on the bluff above Cowlitz Bay*

## 50. Reid Harbor Marsh

**Size and Ownership:** 4.6 acres (State Land managed by Washington State Parks.)

**Facilities:** None in wetland area. [Trails, picnic tables, campsites, drinking water and toilets available nearby.] Dogs must be kept on leash.

**Access:** *By boat:* Located 4.4 nautical miles northwest of the marina at Roche Harbor on San Juan Island, there is a gravelly beach at the head of Reid Harbor that is suitable for landing kayaks and dinghies. Larger boats have the option of using either of the two docks that serve Stuart Island State Park.

Situated at the very head of the harbor, **Reid Harbor Marsh** is a small and often overlooked part of Stuart Island State Park. This 77.5 acre park encompasses a rocky shoreline that supports variety of significant biological features. Growing on the steep slopes along the park's southern shore are scattered individuals of Garry oak (*Quercus garryana*) and several colonies of brittle prickly-pear cactus (*Opuntia fragilis*), including a large patch clinging to the cliff just west of the dock. This rocky shoreline is also one of the best places in the San Juan Archipelago to see wild mink as they forage for small fish and crustaceans along the water's edge. Sometimes river otters are common here too, especially near the marsh.

Framed by the forested dome of Tiptop Hill (the island's highest point), Reid Harbor Marsh is lovely to look at but is much too sensitive for hiking across. The soil here is wet and boggy and it may take several years before a careless boot print is completely erased. Nourished by a forested freshwater wetland that borders its landward edges, the marsh itself becomes increasingly salty the closer it is to the bay. (The gravel berm that physically separates the marsh from the beach still allows sea water to infiltrate into the marsh during high tide.) Consequently, the emergent (open) portions of the marsh are populated with salt-tolerant plants, such as saltgrass (*Distichlis spicata*) and fat hen saltbush (*Atriplex patula*) mixed with species that prefer fresher water such as celery-leaved buttercup (*Ranunculus sceleratus*), one-sided sedge (*Carex unilateralis*) and cinquefoil.

A small grove of about three dozen quaking aspen trees lines the marsh's western border below Tiptop Hill, while along its more publicly-accessed eastern edge, Pacific crabapples dominate. Watch for the occasional red-winged blackbird or marsh wren in late spring and early summer.

*Reid Harbor Marsh*

# Part 7: FIDALGO ISLAND

Many visitors to Anacortes do not realize that they are actually on an island. This landmass, roughly 10 miles long by 8 miles wide, is linked to the mainland by highway bridges at Deception Pass to the South and over Swinomish Channel to the East. Both bridges span rather narrow stretches of dark water, especially Swinomish Channel which describes most of Fidalgo Island's eastern border. The crossings are so brief that you may not realize that you have just left the mainland behind.

The general shape of this 41 square-mile island is largely the result of two large indentations created by Fidalgo and Similk bays. Covering nearly a third of the island's total area, the Swinomish Indian Reservation occupies the entire southeast lobe of the island. The city of Anacortes (population 15,000+) is sited at the island's northern end.

Several large tracts of land have been gifted to the City of Anacortes over time and these have collectively become known as the Anacortes Community Forest Lands (ACFL). Now totaling more than 2,800 acres, the ACFL is administrated by the City for its recreational and conservation values according to a management plan adopted in 1991.

Maps to the entire ACFL are available for purchase from: ACFL, P.O. Box 547, Anacortes, Washington 98221, USA. They can also be obtained in person from the Anacortes Chamber of Commerce. Telephone (360) 293-3832.

# 51. Washington Park

**Size and Ownership:** 292 acres  (City of Anacortes.)

**Facilities:** Trails, picnic tables, campgrounds, drinking water, and toilets.  Dogs must be on leash.

**Access:** From I-5 take Exit 230 and travel west along State Route 20.  After entering Anacortes, go down Commercial Avenue (the main street) and turn left onto 12th Street, following the signs towards the San Juan Islands ferry landing.  At the junction where the road turns downhill on its way to the ferry terminal, continue straight through a set of traffic lights onto Sunset Avenue and proceed to the entrance to the park.  (Roughly three and three-quarters miles from downtown Anacortes.)
*By boat:* There is a public boat-launching ramp and floating dock suitable for most small craft located at Sunset Beach on the north side of the park.

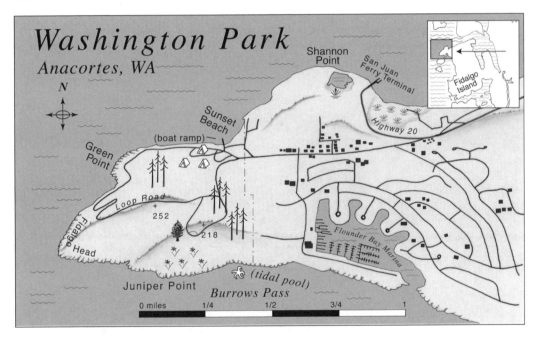

My introduction to **Washington Park** began many years ago.  One night, having missed the late night ferry out to Friday Harbor, I needed to find a place to "crash" until morning.  At sunrise the following day I took a short reconnoitering walk around the park before breaking camp.  But the combination of rocky shore, grassy meadow, and deep coniferous forest proved so beguiling that I elected to stay on for another two days.  Over the years, as I came to know its natural values, this park has consistently revealed itself to be a valuable refuge in many other ways.

Washington Park's piecemeal creation was begun in 1911 when 8 acres of land was donated by Tonjes Havekost, one of Fidalgo Island's early European pioneers. A granite monument to him stands on the park's southern slope overlooking Burrows Pass. In 1913 another 181 acres was added when the city condemned the land for "recreation ground." In 1922 the park was again substantially expanded by the purchase of 75 acres around Green Point. Currently, the park occupies an area roughly a half-mile square (with nearly 2 miles of shoreline). Its highest point is 262 feet above sea level.

A 2.2 mile-long winding scenic drive loops through the park, augmented by more than 2.75 miles of designated hiking trails. Both the road and side trails lead visitors through a variety of habitat types and often provide stunning views of the surrounding islands and sea. (A popular area for early-morning joggers and walkers, the loop road is closed daily to vehicular traffic from 6:00am to 10:00am.)

In the uplands above Green Point (in the park's northwest corner) is a fine woodland dominated by shore pines (*Pinus contorta*). From Juniper Point eastward to

*Steep southern slope of Washington Park facing Burrows Channel*

the park's boundary, the fringing forest above the rocky grasslands consists primarily of a mixture of Douglas fir, Rocky Mountain juniper, and Pacific madrona. Individual specimens of old-growth fir can still be found in the park's interior.

A number of interesting native plants occur within the park: Alaska blueberry (*Vaccinium alaskense*), Sitka alder (*Alnus viridis*), and eight species of ground orchids all have been recorded here. From April through May, the park's rocky meadows support a fine display of spring wildflowers, especially on its southern slopes. The prairie floral list includes yellow monkey flowers, blue-eyed Mary, camas, chocolate lily, Indian paintbrush, death camas, lance-leaved stonecrop, grass widows, Hooker's onion, white fawn lily, Howell's broadiaea and few-flowered shooting star.

The park's most unusual plant, however, may be a small inconspicuous fern known as Indian's dream (*Aspidotis densa*). Also known as pod fern, this stiff 6-to-10-inch tall plant with filigreed leathery leaves is considered to be a reliable indicator species for serpentine soil. Throughout the entire San Juan Archipelago, there are only two places where I know this species is locally abundant: in the open meadows on Mount Constitution and here, where it sends its creeping rhizomes into rocky crevices. (It is especially numerous near the Havekost Memorial.)

*Indian's dream (*Aspidotis densa*)*

In order to properly explain serpentine soil and its actions on plants, I'll need to become rather technical at this point. Serpentine soil is derived from the erosion of

157

serpentine rock and other *ultramafic* minerals. In geologist's terminology, *mafic* rocks are relatively high in iron and magnesium content while being very low in calcium, silica, and aluminum. *Ultramafic* rocks are usually <u>very</u> high in iron and magnesium and, likewise, very low in calcium, etc.. This mineral is created deep underground in the presence of water, which enters the matrix of the parent material. During the process of hydration, it is believed that calcium is lost (from already low levels). Some earth scientists believe that the high levels of calcium found around some sea vents may be part of that calcium expelled during "serpentinization."

The term "serpentine" comes from its resemblance in color to a mottled greenish-brown snake found on serpentine soil in northern Italy. When viewed under a microscope, the greenishness of serpentine soil comes from the millions of tiny fragments eroded from its underlying magnesium silicate-carrying bedrock. (Serpentine soils vary in the darkness of their color according to their iron, chromite, and magnesium content. As much as one-third of the bedrock may be composed of magnesium.)

High levels of magnesium in the soil tend to block a plant's ability to take in soil nutrients, especially calcium. This is especially limiting when calcium and other vital nutrients (such as nitrogen, phosphorus, and molybdenum) are already in very low concentrations. To many species of plants this combination of low calcium and high magnesium can be fatal... but some have been able to cope with these conditions and a few are even considered endemic to serpentine soils. (Identified plant adaptations to serpentine soil have followed at least three primary evolutionary avenues: they can become tolerant of the low calcium-to-magnesium ratio; they can develop high magnesium requirements; or avoid the toxicity by isolating and storing magnesium and other heavy metals within their tissues.) Depending on local and regional geology, the degree of "endemicism" of serpentine soil-adapted plants can range from completely serpentine-restricted to merely partially restricted. Indicator taxa, such as *Aspidotis densa*, are serpentine-restricted in only part of their ranges.

More than one hundred species of birds have been observed in or near Washington Park and the area is considered to be a great place for "winter birding." Some saltwater species include surf scoters, loons, red-necked and western grebes, double-crested and pelagic cormorants, pigeon guillemots, harlequin ducks, rhinoceros auklets, hooded mergansers, brant, and marbled murrelets. Watch along the shoreline for bald eagles and belted kingfishers; in the uplands for pileated woodpeckers, brown creepers, golden-crowned kinglets, dark-eyed juncos and red-breasted nuthatches.

## 52. Cannery Lake

**Size and Ownership:** 18 acres  (Western Washington University.)

**Facilities:** Obscure trail on old railway berm.  [No camping or fires.]  No pets allowed.

**Access:** From downtown Anacortes go west on 12th Avenue, following the signs to the ferry terminal.  Lake is located just west of visitor's parking lot.

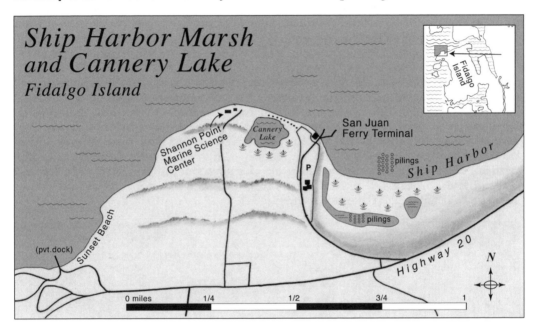

## 53. Ship Harbor Marsh

**Size and Ownership:**  ± 26 acres (Port of Anacortes.)

**Facilities:** Trails.  [No camping.]  Pets must be on leash.

**Access:** From downtown Anacortes go west on 12th Avenue, following the signs to the ferry terminal.  Ship Harbor Marsh is located just east of ferry ticket booths and automobile waiting area.  *By boat:* There are no facilities for larger boats but kayaks and dinghies can be beached in Ship Harbor during periods of high tide.

Here are two natural areas that can be visited while you are waiting for the next available ferry to the outer San Juan Islands. They are both wetland areas that have been heavily impacted and modified by human industry during historical times and are now in the process of being "reclaimed" by nature. **Cannery Lake**, located west of the ferry terminal, is a reservoir that was created by the construction of a berm along its northern side just above the beach. During the first few decades of the 20th Century a railway ran on top of this embankment but it has since been abandoned and its track removed.

Cannery Lake was apparently created from a salt marsh that was backed by forested freshwater wetlands. Its purpose appears to have been to provide a water source for fire-fighting and to supplement the huge fish cannery operation located in nearby Ship Harbor.

Today the lake appears shallow and weed-choked. Its shoreline is wet, marshy, and difficult to negotiate. However, occasional glimpses of the lake can be had from along the old railway berm and from the edge of the ferry parking lot. Muskrats, river otter, deer, raccoons, osprey, and red-winged blackbirds are common in the area. (Yellow perch and brown bullhead catfish have been reported in the lake and probably serve as food for osprey and river otters.) During migration periods, huge flocks of waterfowl may also be seen out on the water. The forested wetland still borders and nurtures the lake's southern shore by providing enough seepage to maintain the reservoir's water level.

*Cannery Lake seen from an abandoned railway berm*

160

**Ship Harbor Marsh** is the former site of a large salmon cannery which operated under various ownerships from 1905 to 1934. By the early 1920s, development of the area around the marsh was extensive. The cannery with its wharves, rail line, warehouses, general store, net sheds, drying racks, mess halls, office building, blacksmith shop, and various other constructions all but obliterated the wetland. Then in the 1930s fish traps were outlawed because of declining fish runs and suddenly the salmon heyday was over. The cannery closed for good.

Years ago, while waiting for the ferry to Friday Harbor, I often explored the old cannery site with its abandoned wharf and large wooden office building that remained a landmark until it was torn down in the 1980s. Now all that remains of the enterprise are dozens of old wooden pilings.

*Pilings from old fishnet drying racks, Ship Harbor Marsh*

Surrounded by development on all landward sides, the marsh is kept separate from the sea by a wide sand/gravel berm. Shell middens on the berm suggest that the area was used as a traditional campsite by local Samish Indians. Most likely this was a saltmarsh before construction of the cannery. Although no paleontologic work has been completed on the site, it appears that the pond (which is freshwater) may have been formed when the berm was enlarged to accommodate the buildings for the cannery.

Realizing the long-term value of this wetland, both historically and ecologically, several local organizations have aided in formally designating this marsh as the "Ship Harbor Interpretive Preserve." Signage explaining the marsh's human and natural history can be found overlooking the area at the edge of the ferry terminal's automobile holding area. Over a thousand feet of beach front invites waiting passengers to climb out of their vehicles and take a walk along its sandy shore.

At present the marsh supports an extensive growth of cattail, interspersed with patches of rush (*Juncus sp*). Surrounding the moist edges of the marsh are vigorous successionary groves of willow and red alder backed by Douglas fir on its southern upland slope.

Great blue herons are frequently seen perched on the decayed pilings of the old wharf or out stalking the shallow water of the bay for small fish during low tide. Red-winged blackbirds, marsh wrens, fox sparrows, and mallard ducks are common back in the marsh.

# 54. Little Cranberry Lake

**Size and Ownership:** ± 35.5 acres (City of Anacortes.)

**Facilities:** Trails. [No camping, drinking water, or toilets.] Dogs must be on leash. Mountain bikes are not allowed on lakeside trails.

**Access:** From Interstate 5 near the town of Burlington, take State Route 20 west to Anacortes. After entering the town turn right onto Commercial Avenue (the main street) and follow it down to 12th Street. Turn left here and follow this route towards the San Juan Island ferries. Turn left onto Georgia Avenue and head straight uphill. Turn right at the Cranberry Lake sign and go to the parking area.

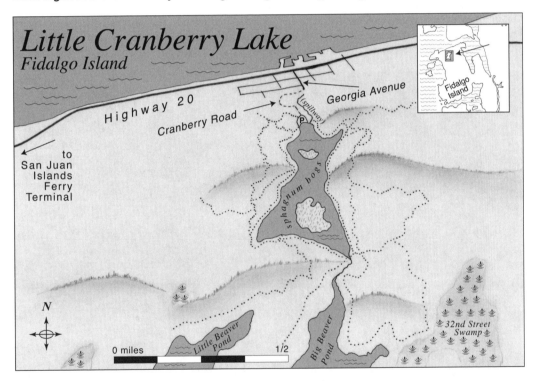

Surrounded by a web of scenic trails, **Little Cranberry Lake** is a popular area for hikers of all ages. It is part of the superbly managed 2,800 acre public reserve known as the Anacortes Community Forest Lands, located in two large parcels in the heart of Fidalgo Island. There is a 1.5 mile loop trail around the lake. (More information about the ACFL can be found on page 193 in the section entitled *"Preserving Natural Areas in the San Juan Islands."*)

Little Cranberry Lake has been deepened into a reservoir by a concrete dam which was constructed at its northern outlet during the 1930s. A previous dam (built in the early 1900s) gave way in 1921 and released a large flood of water that crashed down the half-mile long slope to the beach.

Perched nearly 280 feet above the beach, the lake occupies a basin formed by two forested hills located on either side. Long before the lake was created by the dam, it was essentially a shallow pond partly filled with a large freshwater peat bog. (Some of the peat is apparently several thousand years old.) As the water level rose, the top few feet of the bog (which includes the living portion of the moss mat) broke away from its underlying peat layers and became two floating "islands."

The islands of sphagnum moss can still be seen out in the central areas of the lake's two main lobes. They appear to be well anchored, however, because they do not seem to drift around. But don't try to get out of your boat to walk around on them. The floating matrix may not be able to support your weight and you will most likely

*A tranquil moment at the south end of Little Cranberry Lake*

sink into the water. (This can be extremely dangerous as you may have a very difficult time scrambling back on top the floating mat or into the boat.) It is best to explore the periphery of the bogs by remaining in your canoe or kayak or by examining them through binoculars from shore.

These floating sphagnum mats support a unique mixture of native bog flora which involves nearly a half-dozen kinds of moss. Also present are the carnivorous round-leafed sundew, a white bog orchid (*Platanthera dilatata*), wild cranberry, yellow pond lily, marsh cinquefoil (*Potentilla palustris*), skunk-cabbage, and several small shrubs including swamp laurel (*Kalmia microphylla*), hardhack (*Spiraea douglasii*), and Labrador tea (*Ledum groenlandicum*). There is even a grove of shore pines growing on the largest island, indicating that at least part of this floating matrix is thick and stable enough to support trees, even through windy weather. Numerous seedling trees indicate that this "offshore" forest is spreading.

Wildlife in and around the lake is plentiful and includes wood ducks, Canada geese, belted kingfishers, coyotes, raccoons, river otters, mink, muskrats and the occasional beaver. (Just south of the lake are several large beaver-inhabited ponds.) There are also garter snakes (*Thamnophsis sp.*), Pacific chorus frogs, and the increasingly rare Oregon spotted frog (*Rana pretiosa*), which is currently listed as a endangered species in Washington State. (I was still able to see one, however, during my last visit to the lake.) The "*pretiosa*" portion of this species Latin name means "precious."

Oregon spotted frogs are highly aquatic, living in and around permanent bodies of water. They are most often found in non-woody wetland plant communities. Unfortunately they are also being threatened by a growing population of introduced bullfrogs in Little Cranberry Lake and its neighboring wetlands, such as Big Beaver Pond. (Bullfrogs are known to eat spotted frog tadpoles and adults.) To make matters worse for the spotted frog, bluegills have recently been recorded in the lake. Among various other items, bluegills eat dragonfly larvae - which are thought to be one of the only native predators of bullfrog eggs. This predation boosts the bullfrog's survival rate and may spell the eventual doom for this watershed's spotted frogs.

Little Cranberry Lake's waters also contain crayfish and largemouth bass (according to WDFW records). River otter and mink scats seen near the lake often consist entirely of crayfish shell fragments.

The region around Little Cranberry Lake is said to have been heavily logged between the late 1800s and 1920. However, a few large specimens of old-growth Douglas fir can still be found in some of the area's more inaccessible places. Parts of the mixed second-growth coniferous forest surrounding the lake supports an understory that has dense patches of salal.

# 55. Mount Erie

**Size and Ownership:** ±194 acres  (City of Anacortes.)

**Facilities:** Trails. [No camping, drinking water, or toilets] Dogs must be on a leash.

**Access:** From Interstate 5 near the town of Burlington, take State Route 20 west towards Anacortes. At the major intersection of Sharpe's Corner turn left (south) at the traffic lights to follow the main thoroughfare of State Route 20. After 1.75 miles turn right onto Campbell Lake Road and follow it 1.4 miles to Heart Lake Road. Turn right (north) at the Lake Erie Grocery onto Heart Lake Road. (You will see the massif of Mt. Erie on your right.) The turnoff to Mt. Erie is about 1.75 miles along Heart Lake Road and its another 1.75 miles to the summit by paved road.

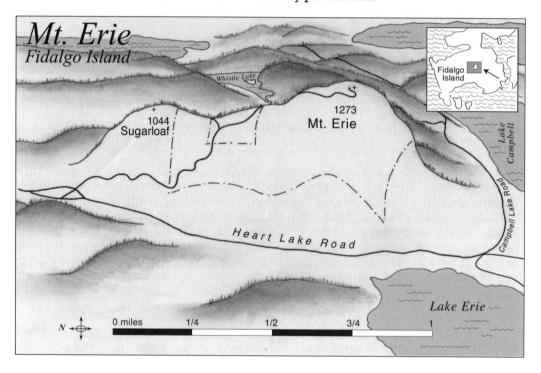

Rising 1,273 feet above sea-level, the unique profile of **Mount Erie** is a landmark visible from many points in the San Juan Islands and as far away as the city of Mount Vernon to the East. The highest spot on Fidalgo Island, Mount Erie's summit offers outstanding vistas of the Olympic and Cascades mountain ranges as well as excellent views of the surrounding lakes and islands. On a clear day you can see Mt. Rainier more than 100 miles away to the South.

Mount Erie and portions of the surrounding area, including nearby Sugarloaf Mountain, is owned by the city of Anacortes. Designated as part of the 2,800 acre Anacortes Community Forest Lands (ACFL), the city has realized that the recreational values of this property far exceeds the market value of the land itself, both in terms of environmental importance and the income generated from recreational and tourist dollars. (More information about the ACFL can be found on page 193 in the section entitled "*Preserving Natural Areas in the San Juan Islands.*")

A large part of Mount Erie is said to be comprised of horneblend and feldspar-rich diorite. Glacial scratches evident on some of the rocky outcrops on the summit are indications that it was completely covered by ice during the last ice-age. Elsewhere over the mountain, most of the glacier-scoured rocks are covered by mantles of thin soil or cushions of moss and lichens. (Some visitors to the area say that Mount Erie is at its best in the spring when its mossy outcroppings are sprinkled with wildflowers.)

The paved road leading to the mountain's top is steep and winding. Down near its beginning, where it turns off from Heart Lake Road, there is a parking area where people can take a forest trail that joins into a rather complex trail system.

*The massif of Mount Erie as seen from the south*

167

A couple of other well-marked trail heads (with parking areas) can also be found along the way to the summit. (The best resource for exploring the trails on and around Mt. Erie is a series of maps available for purchase from ACFL, P.O. Box 547, Anacortes, WA 98221 or in person from the Anacortes Chamber of Commerce or the parks department office located in City Hall.)

The Summit Trail (Trail #26) is rough and steep in places, often passing through thick second-growth forest or squeezing between fern-spattered rock outcrops. Numerous tree stumps indicate that much of the area has been commercially logged in the past, most likely during the middle of the 20th Century. Most of the timber trees now present are of only moderate size, ranging from 6 inches to 2 feet in diameter (DBH) [12 to 14 inch average]. There are, however, occasional large old fire-scarred Douglas firs scattered throughout the forest. In summer, the unique webs of the dome-building spider can be seen nearly everywhere in the understory.

Near the base of the mountain, the wet transitional forest is often dominated by red cedar and a mix of red alder, broad-leaf maple, western hemlock or Douglas fir, especially near where the trail passes small a forested wetland nestled in a rocky depression. Near these places, moisture-loving plants such as willow, lady fern, soft rush, choke cherry, and red elderberry are abundant. As the trail ascends the mountain, hemlock trees become more dominant. At these higher altitudes, sweet coltsfoot (*Petasites frigidus* var. *palmatus*) is occasionally seen. This distinctive plant bears a cluster of large deeply-lobed hand-shaped leaves, each usually supported by a single stem rising directly from the ground.

The Summit Trail comes out at the top of the mountain very close to the communications towers. From the end of the trail it is just a short walk up the road to the overlooks where you will find the view spectacular. Smaller plants such as mountain licorice fern (*Polypodium amorphum*), sedum, kinnikinnik (*Arctostaphylos uva-ursi*), and foamflower (*Tiarella trifoliata*) can be seen growing on the rocks around your feet. Trees in this area include shore pine, hemlock, Douglas fir, and a surprising number of willows. Most willows are associated with wetlands, but up here on the summit, there are hardly any seeps or moist areas. It is very likely, however, that this species' extensive root system is tapping into rainwater trapped deep within the rock fissures.

Whistle Lake is just visible from the summit's eastern overlook. This delta-shaped body of water located in the forest more than 840 feet below and nearly a mile away (as the crow flies) is a popular picnic and swimming spot. Loons, bald eagles and osprey are commonly seen here. Being part of the ACFL, it is accessible from Mount Erie by trail.

Other wildlife common in the Mt. Erie region include chipmunks, Douglas squirrels, black bear, raccoons, turkey vultures, band-tailed pigeons, pileated woodpeckers, dark-eyed juncos, and barred owls.

# 56. Sharpe Park & Montgomery-Duban Headlands

**Size and Ownership:** 112 acres  (Skagit County.)

**Facilities:** Trails, picnic tables, and toilets at parking area.  [No camping.]  Pets must be on a leash.

**Access:** From Interstate 5 near the town of Burlington, take State Route 20 west towards Anacortes.  At the major intersection of Sharpe's Corner turn left (south) at the traffic lights to follow the main thoroughfare of State Route 20 southward for 5 miles, turning right onto Rosario Road at the end of Pass Lake.  (Pass Lake is very close to the highway on your right.)  Continue 1.6 miles up Rosario Road until you see the signed parking area for the park on your left.

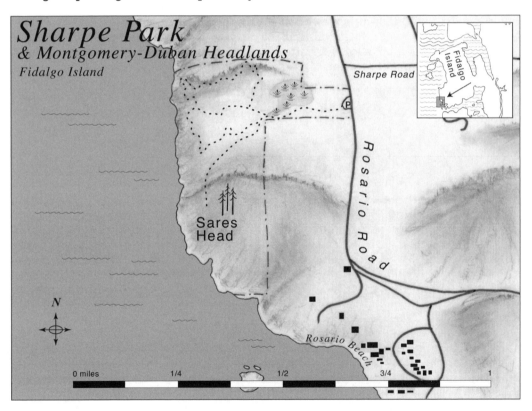

Sharpe Park
& Montgomery-Duban Headlands
Fidalgo Island

Sharpe Road

Fidalgo Island

Rosario Road

Sares Head

N

Rosario Beach

0 miles    1/4    1/2    3/4    1

   **Sharpe Park** was created in 1977 when Kathleen Sharpe donated 75 acres of land to Skagit County.  It included a large freshwater marsh, dense evergreen forest, and Sares Head, a rocky bluff with exceptional views of the surrounding islands.

In 2004, following a two-year-long fundraising campaign led by the San Juan Preservation Trust, an adjacent 37 acre property was purchased and integrated into the county park system. The new property has since been renamed "Montgomery-Duban Headlands Park" in honor of a local family who helped the fundraising effort become successful after it had stalled. Together, the two parks protect nearly three-quarters of a mile of undeveloped saltwater shoreline.

From the parking area, a well-maintained trail passes a large grassy area complete with picnic tables. From here it winds through the moist evergreen forest (dominated by red cedar and Douglas fir) and past an eight-acre freshwater marsh that is home to several species of waterfowl. Just west of this wetland, the trail branches several times but all routes eventually come out onto the rocky heights a couple of hundred feet above Rosario Strait. (There are more than 2.2 miles of linked trails within the two parks.) The most southern segment of this trail system leads to the spectacular 400-foot-high viewpoint at Sares Head.

Watch for bald eagles flying along the shoreline just below you or, every once in a while, right at eye-level.

*View from Sares Head at Sharpe Park*

# Part 8: THE CANADIAN ISLANDS

A group of more than 150 named islands and rocks (some sources say over 300) comprise Canada's southern Gulf Islands. This spectacular region is bounded on the West by Vancouver Island, the Strait of Georgia in the north, and Haro Strait (and the American San Juan Islands) to the East. In the interest of completeness, four of these islands are included in this book. They all meet the criteria for inclusion for listing as a natural area and they all are part of the Salish Sea ecosystem.

In 2003 the Gulf Islands National Park Reserve was created to protect a representation of the Strait of Georgia lowlands bioregion. A patchwork complex involving seven inhabited islands and over 50 smaller islands and emergent rocks, the new park protects some 34 square kilometers (8,400 acres) of land and intertidal zone. Additionally, the sea adjacent to these parklands is protected out to 200 metres (200 yards) offshore. (Until pending land claims by First Nations [indigenous people] are settled, the new park will be called a "National Park Reserve.") Some of the lands included in this national park were formerly part of the British Columbia provincial parks system.

B.C. Ferries provides vehicle and passenger service to Mayne, Saturna, and North & South Pender Islands from Swartz Bay (Vancouver Island) and Tsawwassen (city of Vancouver). All other areas of the park are accessible only by sail or powerboat or kayak. Non-Canadians visiting the region must report to Canadian Customs before proceeding onward to their destination. You are strongly advised to bring your passport for return to the USA. For more information about visiting the park contact:

Gulf Islands National Park Reserve of Canada,
2220 Harbor Road, Sidney, BC, Canada V8L 2P6
Telephone: 250-654-4000  Webpage: http://www.pc.ca/gulf

## 57. D'Arcy Island

**Size and Ownership:** 84 hectares [207.6 acres] (Gulf Islands National Park Reserve Canada.)

**Facilities:** Trails, picnic tables, campsites, and pit toilet. [No drinking water.] Campfires not allowed. Pets must be on leash.

**Access:** *By boat:* D'Arcy Island is located in southern British Columbia on the Canadian side of Haro Strait, about 3.25 miles east of the Saanich Peninsula (Vancouver Island) and 1.25 miles south of Sidney Island. (For those coming from the American side, it is 5.5 nautical miles southwest of Roche Harbor.) Except for a single mooring buoy there are no facilities for larger boats, however kayaks and dinghies can land on a number of gravelly beaches during good weather. A particularly nice landing beach is located along the island's eastern shore near the campground.

173

A wild landscape of rocky coast punctuated by numerous coves and cloaked in a dense forest of Pacific madrona (called "arbutus" in Canada) and Douglas fir, **D'Arcy Island** supports some of the finest forested wetlands to be found on the rocky islands of the Salish Sea. (For most regional Canadians, D'Arcy is considered to be one of the "Gulf Islands.")

Declared a provincial marine park in 1967, D'Arcy Island has a unique human history. From 1891 until 1924, this "escape proof" island was used as a leper colony where members of the Chinese community afflicted with the disease were exiled. A dark chapter in Canadian history, inmates of the island received no medical attention for many years. Their only contact with the outside world was the visit of a ship every three months that brought supplies in the form of food, clothing, gardening supplies, and coffins. In 1924, the federal government closed the leper colony and moved the remaining residents to Bentinck Island where medical facilities were more available. Although the remaining buildings of this sad community were demolished in the 1960s, parts of the old orchard and some concrete ruins still remain.

Even though the inmates of the "leper island" managed to clear nearly five acres of land for their orchard and gardens on the north end of the island, the rest of the forest appears relatively untouched. Most likely, the fear of leprosy prevented wholesale "lumber harvesting" over the entire island during the heyday of the commercial "logger barons" of the late 19th and early 20th centuries.

*Domain of shadows, the northern shore of D'Arcy Island*

174

A trail across the center of the island (beginning near the camping area) leads through some exceptional groves of large trees and forested wetlands. But the "crown-jewel" of habitats can be found as a peripheral wetland that roughly parallels the island's southern shore. Examination of its sediments has revealed that this ecosystem was once a saltmarsh. Due to changes in sea-level and a general buildup of sediments over a time span perhaps as long as 2,200 to 2,500 years or more, the saltmarsh was eventually cut off from direct tidal influence and it slowly transformed into a forested freshwater wetland. Surrounded by native tree species, including quaking aspen, Pacific crabapple, western red cedar, Douglas maple, and various willows, this wetland exhibits little evidence of human disturbance. For example, the large trees that populate its upland watershed areas have never been cut. Consequently the forest soils have not been compacted or otherwise disturbed. Because it is so pristine, in my view this wetland qualifies as the best representative example of this particular kind of habitat in the Salish Sea bioregion.

*One of D'Arcy Island's forested wetlands*

In 2003 D'Arcy Island became part of the Gulf Islands National Park Reserve, one of Canada's newest conservation efforts designed to protect a mosaic of reefs, small islands, rocky headlands, forested hills, wetlands, and accretion shoreforms.

Wildlife observed on the island include black-tailed deer, raccoons, bald eagles, pileated woodpeckers, flickers, fox sparrows, Canada geese, and wandering garter snakes (*Thamnopsis elegans vagrans*). Harbor seals and harlequin ducks are often seen on nearby tidal rocks.

## 58. Sidney Island Spit & Lagoon

**Size and Ownership:** 166 hectares [410 acres] not including intertidal protection zone  (Gulf Islands National Park Reserve Canada.)

**Facilities:** Trails, picnic tables, campsites, drinking water, and toilets.

**Access:** *By boat:* Located 2.1 nautical miles east of the town of Sidney (Vancouver Island) on the Canadian side of Haro Strait, this popular spot is accessible by both private boat and a seasonal walk-on ferry from the town of Sidney.  (For those coming from the American side, it is 7.5 nautical miles west of Roche Harbor.)

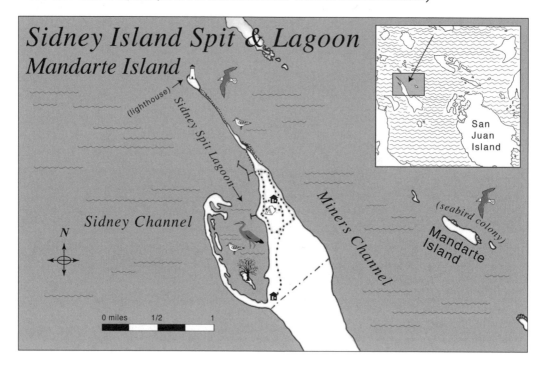

## 59. Mandarte Island

**Size and Ownership:**  ± 6 hectares [± 15 acres]  (Leased by University of British Columbia from Tsawout and Tseuhum Indian Bands.)

**Facilities:** None

**Access:** *By boat:* Mandarte Island is located 2.4 miles southeast of the lighthouse located at the tip of Sidney Island Spit on the Canadian side of Haro Strait.  (For those coming from the American side, it is 5.5 nautical miles west of Roche Harbor on San Juan Island.)  Landing on Mandarte Island is prohibited.

**Sidney Island Spit and Lagoon** provides some of the most important shorebird habitat available in our region, especially during migration periods. Large flocks of brant and Canada geese can be seen utilizing the area during spring, while black oystercatchers, great blue herons, red-breasted mergansers, rhinoceros auklets, pelagic cormorants, double-crested cormorants, glaucous-winged gulls and Heermann's gulls are common in summer and autumn.

The bedrock of the central, northern, and western sections of the island is heavily overlain by layers of clay and unconsolidated glacial sand and gravel deposited, most likely, during the last Ice Age. Constant erosion of this matter from steep-sided "feeder bluffs" situated along the island's northeastern shore apparently provided the material that originally created and presently maintains Sidney Island's long spit. Reaching outward in a northwesterly direction for almost a mile, this narrow bit of land is the most extensive accretion shoreform in the Salish Sea. At low tide, it is the perfect place for a long beachcomber's walk.

Another equally important sandspit branches westward away from the main body of Sidney Island. Somewhat shorter and less picturesque, it extends north and then turns eastward to create and enclose a large shallow saltwater lagoon. Partially exposed during low tides, its sand flats and eelgrass beds are extremely productive

*The long northerly spit of Sidney Island*

177

feeding areas for both shorebirds and diving seabirds (at high tide). Vast numbers of immature Dungeness crabs, bay cockles, lug worms, and small fish occupy this area. In the southern part of the bay sits a tiny rocky islet, known as Eagle Island, that supports a small grove of threatened Garry oak (*Quercus garryana*). Large groups of birds can often be seen resting along the shore at the northern end of the spit. The lagoon is closed to unauthorized boating.

The island's human history includes long use as a summer camp by the Coast Salish Indians, farming by European settlers, and even a spate of industry. Between 1906 and 1915 the Sidney Brick & Tile Company operated here. (Their legacy is now marked by thousands of broken red bricks that litter the shoreline and underbrush.) In 1961 approximately one-third of Sidney Island, including the two sandspits, was designated as a provincial marine park by the British Columbia government. Then in 2003, this increasingly popular natural area's level of protection was dramatically expanded when it became part of Canada's new Gulf Islands National Park Reserve.

As you hike through the partially-forested uplands of this park, you may see fallow deer *(Dama dama)*, an exotic species introduced to neighboring James Island in the early 1900s. During the intervening years, a number of these spotted animals have swum the mile-wide channel across to Sidney Island and established a breeding population. Ecologists are reporting that they have had a dramatic impact on the island's vegetation, particularly the herb and shrub layers, ever since.

The island's forest is dominated by a mixture of Douglas fir, Pacific madrona (arbutus), red cedar, white fir (*Abies grandis*) with scattered growths of broad-leaf maple, yew, and wild cherry. A small grove of quaking aspen (*Populus tremuloides*) is located on the eastern shore of the big lagoon. (Growing just a few feet from saltwater, this is a very unusual site to encounter this species. Perhaps this particular clone is exceptionally salt-tolerant.)

Other wildlife commonly seen in the park include bald eagles, wild turkeys, rufus hummingbirds, introduced Javanese peafowl, black-tailed deer, fox sparrows, dark-eyed juncos, turkey vultures, Steller's jays, pileated woodpeckers, Douglas squirrels, and harbor seals (hauled out at the end of the spit near the lighthouse).

Please note that while local drinking water is available (except when the well occasionally runs dry in late summer) it has a high sodium content and should not be consumed by persons with kidney or heart ailments. If in doubt, bring along your own water supplies.

During winter almost all of the park is closed to public use (except the spit itself) from November until February. During this period, First Nations (Native) people hunt the numerous fallow deer on the island.

When you first see it by boat or air from the south, the rocky cliffs of **Mandarte Island** appear to be almost pure white in color. Upon closer examination the reason soon becomes apparent: they are stained with guano from the thousands of seabirds nesting there. With some 8,000 to 10,000 birds nesting annually on the island, this is the largest seabird colony in the Salish Sea. The primary species here include pelagic cormorants, double-crested cormorants, pigeon guillemots, and glaucous-winged gulls. But this spot is also one of the few places in the region where tufted puffins and Brandt's cormorants can occasionally still be seen.

Located only a mile or so east of Sidney Island, out in Miner's Channel, this little island (named after Father Mandarte, the first Roman Catholic priest to arrive on the Saanich Peninsula) is well worth making a trip to see. Be aware, however, that you will <u>not</u> be allowed to land and you must not approach the island closer than one hundred meters (about 100 yards). During the nesting season - spring through early autumn - the University of British Columbia's research station (a collection of shacks located on the island's northeast end) are occupied by busy scientists and students.

Over the years, several benchmark studies of birds have been conducted here. Back in 1960 a long-term study of the small resident population of song sparrows (*Melospiza melodia*) [a land-bird] was begun on this isolated island. (The sparrow population was small enough that every individual could be uniquely marked and their survival and reproduction monitored over many generations.) A great deal has been learned since then, such as the effects of population crashes caused by severe winter weather and nest parasitism by brown-headed cowbirds.

*Cormorants nesting on Mandarte Island*

But, interestingly, these birds have not shown any advance in breeding dates as a response to global warming. (Spring is supposedly coming earlier each year.) However, these studies have indicated that the sparrow population does exhibit considerable annual variation in breeding times that seem correlated with the arrival of the El Niño Southern Oscillation. These birds apparently breed earlier in warmer El Niño years and later in colder La Niña years.

Another study looked at the northwestern crow, a major predator and scavenger in local seabird colonies. On Mandarte Island they were found to consume 22% of all eggs laid in the first clutches of both double-crested and pelagic cormorants. They also prey on newly hatched young cormorants. But when boats or visiting people come too close, the added disturbance can cause the parent birds to fly away in alarm, leaving the nests unprotected. You can be sure that the sharp-eyed crows will take advantage of the situation and raid the nests. In this way the number of young produced by a seabird colony can be heavily influenced by human disturbance.

Seabirds can also be strongly affected by certain insecticides, such as DDT, or industrial chemicals, such as PCBs. Due to bioaccumulation, levels of some of these contaminants in the eggs of fish-eating birds, such as cormorants, may be as high as 25 million times the concentrations found in the waters in which the fish live. This can cause congenital deformities and poor nesting success due to thin egg shells.

Fortunately the level of toxins found in the Salish Sea appears to have declined substantially since the 1970s when serious monitoring was begun. In part this is the result of outlawing DDT (and its derivatives) and to improvements in the regulation of pulp and paper mill effluents. The bad news is that a Canadian survey done in 2000 has shown that the cormorants living in our region have continued to decline alarmingly. This has prompted a "red listing" of the double-crested cormorant by the British Columbia government and its federal listing as a "species of concern." It is evident that persistent toxic chemicals are still in the marine environment and in the animals that live there. We still have a lot of work to do before it is cleaned up.

## 60. Rum Island (Isle-de-lis)

**Size and Ownership:** 4.7 hectares [11.6 acres] (Gulf Islands National Park Reserve Canada.)

**Facilities:** Trails, picnic tables, campsites, and pit toilets. [No drinking water] Pets must be on leash.

**Access:** *By boat:* Rum Island is located in southern British Columbia on the Canadian side of Haro Strait, about 4.75 miles east of the town of Sidney (Vancouver Island) and 2.4 miles northeast of Sidney Island. (For those coming from the American side, it is 5.8 nautical miles northwest of Roche Harbor.) There are no facilities for larger boats but kayaks and dinghies can land on the northern side of the gravelly isthmus that connects Rum Island to neighboring Gooch Island.

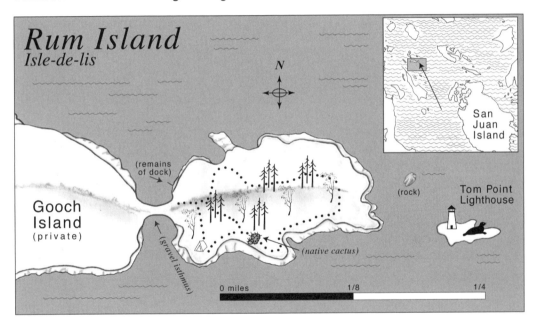

Rum Island received its name from its former role as a base for smuggling prohibited spirits into the United States during the prohibition era of the 1920s. The island became a marine park in 1971, following its donation to the Province by the Maccaud-Nelson family. It was specified that it be called "**Isle-de-lis**" (French for "Island of Lilies") for the wild lilies that grow there - hence the two names for the island. In 2003, Isle-de-lis Marine Park was incorporated into Canada's Gulf Islands National Park Reserve.

Geologically speaking, Isle-de-lis (Rum Island) consists primarily of sandstone interbedded with a conglomerate of water-worn pebbles and rocks. The island's picturesque shoreline is lined with sea-sculptured sandstone forms and deeply indented "pocket coves." It is linked to its nearest neighbor, Gooch Island, by an accretion of gravel which forms a short isthmus approximately 25 feet wide and 100 feet long (7.6m x 30.48m). The island is covered with pockets of thin welled-drained soil that support a relatively undisturbed forest dominated by Douglas fir, shore pine, and Pacific madrona (arbutus). In places where the soil becomes too thin to promote woody growth there are small patches of native grasses, sedums, various lilies, and even a few colonies of the rare brittle cactus (*Opuntia fragilis*).

A casual trail circles the island, providing stunning views of Haro Strait and the surrounding islands. Watch for seals and river otters on the nearshore rocks around Tom Point, at the island's eastern end. Fringing the island here, just offshore, is an extensive "forest" of bull kelp (*Nereocystis luetkeana*). This giant brown algae can grow up to about 80 feet (24.4m) in length and forms a critical link in the ecology of the Salish Sea. Small fish take shelter in the canopy created by these kelp forests, while countless tiny creatures consume the kelp itself, especially at the end of its summer growing cycle.

*Bull kelp forest flanking the east end of Rum Island (Isle-de-lis)*

# Part 9: PRESERVING NATURAL AREAS IN THE SAN JUAN ISLANDS

Most of the natural areas described in this book were chosen because they either contain unique biological features or support ecological functions that create critical habitats for certain vulnerable species of native flora and fauna. These sixty sites were selected from over two hundred potential locations that when carefully examined also met other criteria for inclusion. For example, they all needed to have some level of public access available, even if only by written permission. They also must have some kind of intrinsic protection. In effect, they had to be able to bear up to what I call "visitor erosion." Some of the sites that I have included in this list have natural moats that separate visitors from the truly sensitive areas and prevent casual trespass; others have durable established trails and visiting hours. A few exceptional places are continually monitored by caretakers, rangers, or other interested people.

Even though all of these places qualify as important natural areas, it does not mean that they are truly pristine. During my many years of local research and habitat assessment here in the San Juan Islands, I have only found one site larger than a half of an acre that does not bear testimony of human activity. Some of the evidence is prehistoric and can only be inferred by the presence of a remnant oak savannah or grassland/forb community that was maintained for hundreds, if not thousands of years, by native people purposely burning the land to clear it of unwanted growth and encourage food-rich ecosystems.

In truth, if it were not for this yearly "fire stick farming" ritual carried out by native people until the mid-nineteenth century, most of our open habitats would have been swallowed up by the forest long ago. Much of it is again in danger of being lost because we have prevented the burning for so long. Unfortunately, when these neglected habitats do experience wildfire, they often burn too intensely because of an over-accumulation of fuel, destroying the savannah or native grassland itself and even threatening our homes.

Those early people left lots of other evidence about their activities. Many of their old campsites are littered with deep layers of discarded whelk, oyster, and clam shells (midden) that indicate centuries of seasonal (and sometimes permanent) occupation. Poking around in some of those old spots, I have discovered Neolithic arrowheads and stone grinding tools incongruously mixed in with pieces of rusted barbed wire. Heralding the settlement by Europeans, bits of fencing wire and broken bottles are some of the most common and widespread artifacts to be found littering the soils of former pioneer farms.

The Europeans also changed the shape and function of the landscape, often in dramatic ways. They dug ponds, drained wetlands, plowed meadows, logged and cleared forest to create pastures, brought in cattle and sheep to graze those pastures, introduced exotic orchard and garden plants (and their attendant weeds), gouged roads out of the hillsides, built homes, constructed offices and stores, and created the towns and early infrastructure of our spreading civilization.

Even though signs of human activity are evident in virtually every rocky cranny and hidden wetland throughout the islands (and most of the mainland) and even if some ecosystems are strained to the limit by our interference and pollution, I am still continually amazed at the durability of our natural systems and how quickly nature will "reclaim" a landscape once a disturbance has stopped. A good example of this can be seen at Lime Kiln Quarry on San Juan Island. For decades it was an industrial site, its bedrock blasted with dynamite and scraped by bulldozers and other huge machines. But within only a year or two after the cessation of commercial activity, shallow wetlands began to form in its low impervious spots. Those wetlands have now become important breeding areas for some forms of increasingly rare frogs. Specialized plants have also colonized the area — some in those wet areas, others on the manmade rocky cliffs — each according to its needs. Presently every year, on one of the quarry's compacted and abandoned "haul" roads, appears the most spectacular springtime bloom display of Calypso orchids that I have ever seen.

## A Problem of Nature

Unfortunately, just leaving things alone is not always enough. Also, we do not always have the option of this "laissez-faire" attitude. Human beings live here, as we have a right to, but it's just that there are so many of us and our numbers are still increasing. The cumulative impact of our tireless activities, begun with that first digging stick many millennia ago and now evolved into bulldozers, deep sea trawlers, and jumbo jets, is becoming readily apparent. We are witnessing global, regional, and local environmental changes and conditions that are the sum result of millions, perhaps billions, of small incremental events that have occurred, mostly unnoticed, year after year.

Just have a quick look at a daily newspaper. Today we are faced with the prospect of global warming, with dire predictions about associated changes in climate. Marine and aquatic ecosystems are being systemically polluted with the persistent residues of industrial processes including polychlorinated biphenyls and pesticides that threaten wildlife because they concentrate in body tissues. The constant erosion of critical habitats and the spread of invasive species (nearly one-third of the 800+ plant species found in the San Juan Islands are exotics) are restricting and may eventually eliminate dozens, perhaps hundreds, of species of native plants and animals. These are just the things that are being reported; there are many many more small unheralded changes that contribute to this slow ecological decline.

## Our Responses to Environmental Change

In our local communities, we are seeing continuously increased restrictions in nearly every aspect of our personal lives. We now need permits and licenses (along with their associated rules and regulations) to catch a fish, sleep in a park, build a bonfire, dig for drinking water, water the lawn, build a shed, drive a car, park that car, fell a tree, or even to walk your dog. Do these governing regulations sub-stantially aid in the long-term maintenance of our natural resources and environ-ment? I doubt it. Most of them appear to be simply reactions to perceived social problems and (ultimately) another source of public revenue. They merely allow us to look like we're doing something constructive... at least on paper.

Even when focusing on the subject of environmental change, as many scientists have, it's not easy to chart the day-by-day incremental permutations that are slowly depleting our natural heritage. (It's really a lot like watching a kind of slow-motion evolution.) Most of us lose track of these changes and seldom notice that anything is amiss until there is a crisis somewhere in the system. Why is this? Perhaps it is because none of us are born with a sense of corruption. To a small child the world is something new and wonderful and it makes perfect sense to accept the state of it as "normal" as we grow up, even if our environment has in reality become a little more impoverished with each new generation. In spite of our increasing aware-ness of the world around us as we mature, our "baseline" is always still our own personal beginning.

Another factor that affects our perception of environmental change is that we move around a great deal. According to one statistic that I recently saw, the average stay in a particular home for the "average" American family is just four years - not a lot of time in which to track long-term environmental changes in your neighborhood. But just four years is plenty enough time for us to be able to see *some* changes: a new house on that vacant lot, a new shopping center just around the corner, a widened road over there. In response, we modern people spend a lot of energy trying to escape the pressures of our work and home environment through vacations and weekend outdoor recreation. But one day, as you sit in your boat at your favorite fishing spot, you might remember how gratifying the fishing was here just ten years ago and for some strange reason you haven't had a bite for two days. You might even wonder how good was fishing at this spot fifty years ago? ... or a hundred years ago? ... but now there seems nothing else to do but to shrug it off and check your bait.

Should we just give up in face of these apparently overwhelming prospects? If I were a fatalist, I would say, "Yes! Just let nature take its course and all of us along with it." But I refuse to go down without a fight... and I hope that you will agree that we owe it to ourselves, or at least to our children, to not give up. We still may lose out in the long-run, but our efforts today will at least serve to improve the quality of our own lives and perhaps extend the length of our grandchildren's as well.

We need to discover better ways to bring our time and endeavors together. Ever since visionary leaders such as John Muir and Aldo Leopold guided the early days of the so-called "environmental movement" during the late 19th and early 20th centuries, there has been a very noticeable effort to legislate conservation both in the USA and Canada. Here in our island archipelago, no fewer than 28 government agencies (including the US Fish and Wildlife Service, the US National Park Service, Washington Department of Natural Resources, Washington Department of Ecology, British Columbia Provincial Parks, National Parks Canada, Canada's Department of Fisheries & Oceans, and more...) claim jurisdiction over an equally bewildering mosaic of land parcels, habitats, and even individual species.

Is this hodge-podge of governing agencies, often replete with conflicting policies, our best shot out of our predicament? Can a combination of ever-increasing authority and compliance be a strong enough force to aid the natural world in healing itself? Maybe. But more likely it was this very hodge-podge coupled with our civilization's sense of manifest destiny (our <u>right</u> to "use" the earth and its natural resources) that got us into this cumbersome disconnected mess in the first place. If this is true, what can we do that would amount to effective conservation?

## Thinking Outside of Our Box

Fortunately, a lot of people who work for the "hodge-podge" are realizing just how helpless they really are to accomplish what needs to be done. They have seen their budgets trimmed year after year - in some cases dramatically. Or, they have suddenly been mandated with new priorities, such as national security, that divert their limited resources away from protecting the natural environment. With limited ability to reach across property ownership boundaries many well-meaning land managers have watched, dismayed down to their very being, as their best efforts consistently collapse far short of the mark. Under circumstances such as these, I can see how easy it would be to become discouraged. But in the long run these adversities and failures may actually be helping to make future conservation efforts more effective. They are forcing government agencies to develop cooperative strategies with other members of the "hodge-podge" and with other interested parties (the stakeholders) like you and me.

In most cases, the lines that we draw to delineate the boundaries of our properties do not follow natural borders; human land ownership is an arbitrary overlay on the map and in the landscape. This poses complications for anyone trying to be a responsible land steward. Here is a story based on an actual case: A man lives on an eleven-acre property that contains an old farmhouse. The original farm had been subdivided at least twice and now his property line goes through the middle of a wetland surrounded by forest. As steward to this lovely natural area, how can he manage and protect just *half* of a wetland? Any invasive weeds that he might remove, such as reed canarygrass (*Phalaris arundinacea*) which can severely restrict the biodiversity in a wetland, would almost instantly be restocked by the seed bank created by the plants that remained on his neighbor's half.

Now let's have a closer look at that wetland choked with reed canarygrass. There is good evidence indicating that this species of invasive grass can largely be removed by several years of inundation. In other words, simply raising the water level in our wetland would cause most of the canarygrass to drown. The odd remaining plant could then be dealt with by grubbing it out mechanically or with a judicious spot of non-systemic herbicide. Once the reed canarygrass is gone, the water level could be brought back to "normal" and hopefully the wetland would be healed and its natural biodiversity should increase.

But all of the above can happen only if the man's neighbor agrees to his plan and willingly cooperates. To be perfectly legal, the plan would also need the blessings of the local County Planning Department, and the Department of Fish and Wildlife (especially if there were baby salmon in the outlet stream), and the Department of Natural Resources (if a permanent watercourse or timber trees were involved), and the Department of Ecology, and the Army Corps of Engineers, and the Office of the... well, I might be exaggerating this slightly but you get the message. Faced with such a gauntlet of required permits there is little wonder why a person would not attempt such a bodacious act as fixing a wetland. Even though we know exactly what needs to be done for the wetland and have even worked out the most effortless method of attaining that goal, we are intimidated and blocked by the "hodge-podge" of bureaucracy. Taking personal responsibility as a steward of the environment is not going to move ahead in this scene.

Okay... let's go back and have yet another look at that same wetland divided by property lines. Let's say a different neighbor has offered to donate his corner of it to a conservation organization (such as the San Juan County Land Bank, the San Juan Preservation Trust, or even the Washington Department of Fish and Wildlife). A site assessment made by the agency in question would reveal that the donated parcel is a bit small and that the entire wetland, which was once was an important contributor to the local ecology, has now been severely degraded. At this point most conservation organizations would very likely pass on acquiring it: best not to spread one's limited resources too thin.

Hang on! This was once a highly diverse wetland with an important ecological function. Instead of giving it a miss, let's say an enlightened manager from one of those agencies sees our wetland's full potential. So we have a series of neighborhood meetings and soon begin to make cooperative agreements with each other. The conservation agency promises to coordinate the legal process, clearing the "permit path" while seeking a little funding. The community responds by chipping in with a bit of cash and some "elbow-grease" to restore the degraded wetland.

Decisively, a temporary coffer dam is constructed and soon the inundated canarygrass is looking rather sad. Three years later the dam is breached, and the wetland slowly returns to normal. The reed canarygrass is now gone and we are amazed at the influx of wildlife. To top it off, we discover a rare wetland plant which hasn't been seen anywhere on the island in decades. Sweet! Does all this sound like just wishful thinking? Well, it isn't. I have since relocated from that eleven acre property but the wetland and its little bog plant actually exist and continue to do fine to this day. The identity of my former neighborhood and the contributing agency have been deliberately obscured for purposes of privacy.

Land and natural resource managers are just beginning to realize the incredible potential of cooperative strategies. Since the key word here is "co-operative," it implies community participation on both large and small scales. Of course it won't all be smooth sailing. There will always be those who object and obstruct, but the ideal of "community will" may prove in the long run to be our best hope for a real future. We also need to couple this with real incentives. For example, many landowners are seeking property tax relief because they maintain wildlife habitats on their land. The county code has a provision regarding property tax relief, but the administrators claim that they cannot afford to grant relief to all landowners. Perhaps in the near future (hopefully before we are in crisis) we will see generous property tax reductions for folks who are willing to put their properties (of almost any size) into a countywide habitat conservation program.

The truth is becoming increasingly apparent: conservation goals cannot be met by simply setting aside parcels of land, no matter how large they may be. Few of the natural areas described in this book, for example, are large enough to ensure the conservation of any complete ecosystem, especially when essential processes that create and maintain that system are located at a distance upstream. We need to have cooperative agreements with neighboring landowners in order to put all of the pieces of the puzzle together. In this way, entire wetlands, watersheds, travel corridors, and important ecotones can be protected and even enhanced. To be effective, these agreements must also be part of an ongoing long-term vision. If we wish to continue to have natural areas we absolutely cannot afford to let them stand alone and unattended. It takes vigilance and effort to preserve the essence of the San Juan Islands but almost without exception when we take the trouble to do it, both the natural landscape and our personal lives benefit immeasurably.

# Cooperative Conservation Resource Guide  (*What You Can Do*)

The following is an incomplete but hopefully useful list of organizations (government and non-government) that are working towards habitat and wildlife conservation in the San Juan Archipelago.  Some of these agencies will consider cooperative agreements with landowners who have properties that border lands managed by them.  Others have programs for volunteers who want to "lend a hand" in a meaningful way.  All employ key people who are open to discuss new ideas:

- **The San Juan Preservation Trust  (SJPT)**
  The San Juan Preservation Trust is perhaps the most active non-government conservation organization (NGO) in the San Juan Islands.  Created in 1979, (making it the oldest conservation land trust in the State) it now owns or manages under conservation agreements more than 12,000 acres of land on 18 islands.  For more information visit their website at: http://www.sjpt.org/ or call their office (360) 468-3202.

- **San Juan County Land Bank**
  This county agency is the only public land bank in Washington State.  Created in 1991, its mandate is "to preserve in perpetuity areas in the County that have environmental, agricultural, aesthetic, cultural, scientific, historic, scenic or low-intensity recreational value, and to protect existing and future sources of potable water."  Working primarily within a limited budget financed by a 1% tax on local real estate sales, their land-acquisition program has been very robust and the Land Bank currently manages more than 4,750 acres of county-owned preserves and private lands that are licensed with conservation agreements.  The Land Bank also has an active volunteer program to maintain and "keep an eye" on specific preserves.  For more information phone (360) 378-4402 or visit their website at: http://www.co.san-juan.wa.us/land_bank/

- **Washington State Department of Natural Resources (DNR)**
  The passage of the Natural Area Preserves Act in 1972 paved the way for the development of a statewide system of state-owned natural areas. The DNR was authorized to establish and manage this system.  There are now several Natural Area Preserves within the San Juan Islands.  In 1981, the Natural Areas Preserves Act was amended in order to establish a Natural Heritage Program within the DNR.  This opened the way for developing a scientific approach to the process of identifying candidate sites for the natural areas system.  Since then, the Natural Heritage Program's role has been broadened to collect archival information about all the State's native ecosystems and rare species and to distribute that information to other conservation agencies and to the public.  For more information please visit the following websites:
  Natural Heritage Program: http://www.dnr.wa.gov/nhp/index.html
  Natural Area Program: http://www.dnr.wa.gov/nap/index.html

- **Washington State Parks and Recreation Commission**
The "Commission" is charged by the citizens of Washington to "protect a diverse system of recreational, cultural, historical and natural sites." Much of the park system has received limited development and approximately 85-90% may be classified as "resource recreation" or "natural areas" (Natural Areas, Natural Forest Areas, or Natural Area Preserves); land-uses that afford a high degree of protection to native flora and fauna. To safeguard the public lands in its trust, the State Parks resource stewardship program administers a broad range of conservation activities, including the inventory and assessment of natural and cultural resources, management planning, applied research, stewardship training and special topics of statewide significance such as salmon recovery. For local information telephone Lime Kiln State Park (San Juan Island) at
(360) 378-2044 or Moran State Park (Orcas Island) at (360) 376-2326.
To learn more about the park system and its programs visit their web site at: http://www.parks.wa.gov

- **Friends of the San Juan Islands**
"Friends" is a nonprofit organization that's been around for more than a quarter of a century. For many years its role was primarily the "watchdog" of development in the islands (both commercial and private) and of the actions of local government. Nowadays it also maintains an vigorous program in shoreline protection. They have an active team of volunteers who assist with activities that benefit nearshore habitats such as beach restoration and field studies with staff to monitor for invasive species such as spartina grass and green crabs. They also help in community beach "cleanups" each spring and fall. For more information telephone their office in Friday Harbor at (360) 378-2319 or visit their website at: http://www.sanjuans.org

- **The Nature Conservancy of Washington (TNC)**
Founded in 1951, TNC presently has about 1 million members and supporters with operations in all 50 states and in more than 30 countries. The organization maintains a number of preserves in the San Juan Islands, two of which (Yellow Island and Cowlitz Bay) are featured in this book. The TNC also has an active collaboration program with volunteers and other agencies to help protect shoreline environments. For more information please call their Seattle office at (206) 343-4344 or e-mail them at: washington@tnc.org
The addresses to their websites are: http://www.tnc.org/washington
http://www.nature.org/wherewework/northamerica/states/washington/

- **San Juan Island National Historical Park**
Originally gazetted in 1966 to preserve evidence of occupation by British and American troops during a formative period of US history, the park's two units (totaling some 1,752 acres) contain exceptionally diverse natural habitats and rare species. Biodiversity is high within the park. For instance, 34 species of butterflies have been recorded there, including at least one endangered variety.

Garry oak woodland and native prairie restoration programs are well under way. The park's managers also coordinate an active volunteer program with jobs that range from park hosts and natural history interpreters, to colorful roles in historical reenactments. For more information call: (360) 378-2240 or visit the website for San Juan Island National Historical Park at: http://www.nps.gov/sajh/

- **United States Fish and Wildlife Service (USFWS)**
  Some 83 rocky reefs and islands totaling almost 450 acres in the San Juan Island Archipelago have been designated as the San Juan Islands National Wildlife Refuge. Additionally, most of these islands have been tagged by Congress as a wilderness area where seabirds, eagles, and marine mammals can have an undisturbed place to live and raise their young. Management of the refuge is the responsibility of USFWS. All the refuge islands except Turn Island and Matia Island (which are featured in this book) are closed to the public. For more info about the role of USFWS in the San Juan Islands, telephone their regional office in Port Angeles at (360) 457-8451. The websites for the refuge can be viewed at:
  http://www.fws.gov/pacific/refuges/field/wa_sanjuanis.htm
  http://www.fws.gov/refuges/profiles/

- **Washington Department of Fish and Wildlife (WDFW)**
  WDFW has limited authority to protect habitat on other than state-owned lands, so they work collaboratively with land managers and landowners through numerous strategies including incentives, easements, agreements, acquisitions and technical assistance on best management practices and habitat restoration. In addition, WDFW has the authority to regulate activities within fish-bearing waters, and the importation and release of aquatic and terrestrial animal species and aquatic plants. Visit the following website links for more information about WDFW programs which include nearshore protection, salmon recovery, grants and technical assistance:
  Habitat Protection & Wildlife Areas: http://wdfw.wa.gov/habitat.htm
  Backyard Wildlife Sanctuary Program: http://wdfw.wa.gov/wlm/byw_prog.htm
  Landscaping for Wildlife: http://wdfw.wa.gov/wlm/landscap.htm

- **Washington Department of Ecology (DOE)**
  The Department of Ecology has long been considered the "heavy" for enforcement of a wide variety environmental regulations ranging from sewage disposal, underground storage tanks, well drilling, use of wood stoves, oil spills, automotive repair shops, and building demolition. In order to counter this negative image, the agency is also conducting a public outreach program that provides technical assistance to help support voluntary compliance with environmental rules and promote good stewardship of environmental resources.

  The Shorelands & Environmental Assistance Program, for example, works to protect wetland habitat and native plants through a joint effort between the Washington Conservation Corps and DOE's Wetlands Protection Unit. The Conservation Corps mobilizes youth teams to work in watershed recovery and restoration. DOE's homepage with links to program information can found at the following web address: http://www.ecy.wa.gov/ecyhome.html

- **San Juan County Noxious Weed Control Board**
  Non-native invasive plant species are thought to be the second greatest threat to natural ecosystems following direct habitat loss. The mission of the San Juan County Noxious Weed Control Board is to serve as a responsible land steward by striving to eradicate new invasions and prevent the spread of already established noxious non-native weeds. Their coordinators and volunteers advise citizens about noxious weed control and make printed educational materials readily available. Also of interest is an ongoing biocontrol program (in cooperation with Washington State University) that uses insects to eat specific weeds, including meadow knapweed, tansy ragwort, and purple loosestrife.
  For more information call (360) 376-3499 or visit their webpage at:
  http://sanjuan.wsu.edu/noxious/index.html

- **United States Bureau of Land Management (BLM)**
  Around 1,000 acres of federal lands in the San Juan islands are managed by the BLM (Spokane District, Wenatchee Resource Area). A large part of these diverse properties, which are mostly located on southern Lopez Island, have been designated as Areas of Critical Environmental Concern (ACEC). Until rather recently the agency played the role of "absentee landlord." Unfortunately this neglect has also allowed woody shrubs and exotic plants to invade native grasslands and wetlands. Their recent focus on rectifying some of these management problems has led to an increased presence in the San Juans and some interesting ventures. One such enterprise (completely refurbishing the long-neglected Turn Point lightkeeper's complex on Stuart Island) is providing the agency with a charming venue for public education and outdoor experience programs. BLM presently maintains a one-person office on Lopez Island. You may telephone the agency's local representative at (360) 468-3754 or send a letter to: BLM, P.O. Box 3, Lopez Island, WA 98261.

- **San Juan Islands Conservation District**
  This is our local conservation district with an office located in Friday Harbor on San Juan Island. Funded primarily through grants provided by the Washington State Conservation Commission (and a variety of other sources including property tax) this agency works to promote conservation of the county's natural resources by providing free information and technical assistance to any citizen or organization that makes a request. Services offered include native plant use and wildlife habitat preservation, low impact development strategies, sustainable farm and forest resource planning, water quality and watershed assessments, and natural resource education workshops.
  For more information call (360) 378-6621 or visit their website at:
  http://www.sanjuanislandscd.org/index.html

- **Natural Resources Conservation Service (NRCS)**
  The NRCS is an informational and public outreach agency of the US Department of Agriculture. NRCS and its partners, such as local conservation districts and Native American Indian tribes, utilize volunteers to help create wildlife awareness, promote local conservation projects, and educate the community on habitat needs and conservation strategies. Each year, in Washington State alone, an "army" of 1,500 to 2,000 volunteers assist the NRCS towards these goals. With a local office in nearby Mount Vernon, the NRCS is becoming increasingly active in the San Juan Islands. For more information about NRCS programs, including conservation grants, call them at (360) 428-7684 or visit their Washington State website at: http://www.wa.nrcs.usda.gov/

- **Washington Native Plant Society (WNPS)**
  A nonprofit organization with local chapters state-wide (including the San Juan Islands), members of WNPS share a common interest in Washington's unique flora. This society has been active for more than 30 years with numerous research projects and educational activities being supported by Society funds. Highlighting their commitment to protecting native plants, the society's Native Plant Stewardship Program (an annual workshop offered in the central Puget Sound region) provides training on the importance and use of native plants in restoration and landscaping. In return for this training, Native Plant Stewards contribute volunteer service in community education, habitat protection, and habitat restoration. Field trips, study weekends and regular program meetings are offered to Society members. For more information call their toll-free number: 1-888-288-8022 or visit their webpage at: http://www.wnps.org/

- **Anacortes Community Forest Lands (ACFL)**
  Although the business leaders of Anacortes may complain (loudly at times) that their small city has not become the region's commercial center, in reality this is one very lucky community. Long regarded as the "Gateway to the San Juan Islands," Anacortes has also had the very good fortune to inherit Washington Park (with its exquisite shoreline and upland habitats) and several nearby large tracts of biodiverse property called the Anacortes Community Forest Lands. Totaling some 2,800 acres, the ACFL includes Mount Erie, Whistle Lake, Little Cranberry Lake, and Heart Lake. Properly managed with an eye to the future, the City is slowly discovering that these lands are becoming priceless treasures to the community. Not only does the ACFL and Washington Park help preserve some significant watersheds and critical native plant and wildlife habitats, it is fast becoming an important recreation destination for locals and visitors alike. The ACFL is managed by the Anacortes Parks and Recreation Department located at City Hall. For more information or to acquire maps of the ACFL's 50 miles of multiple-use trails, call (360) 293-1918 or visit their website at: http://www.cityofanacortes.org/parks.asp

  Friends of the Forest is a nonprofit organization dedicated to the preservation of the ACFL through education, outreach, and stewardship. Formed in 1987, "The Friends" were integral to the creation of a conservation easement program that ultimately will protect 1,500 acres of ACFL that was potentially vulnerable to commercial logging to help city revenues. Under this ongoing program, for every $1,000 donated to the City's Forest Land Endowment Fund one acre is placed in a conservation easement with the Skagit Land Trust that prohibits logging, mining, commercial development, or its sale or lease. For more information about the activities of "The Friends" visit their website at: http://www.friendsoftheacfl.org/

- **Gulf Islands National Park Reserve (Parks Canada)**
  One of Canada's newest conservation efforts to protect a mosaic of reefs, small islands, rocky headlands, forested hills, wetlands, and accretion shoreforms in the Salish Sea Bioregion. The park's staff run a small volunteer program that primarily targets the removal of invasive weedy plants such as Scots broom. This might be a excellent way to have an intimate look at some exceptional sites. For more information call (250) 654-4000 and ask for the volunteers coordinator or visit their webpage at: http://www.pc.ca/gulf

- **Garry Oak Ecosystems Recovery Team (GOERT)**
  A nonprofit organization dedicated to the recovery of Garry oak and associated ecosystems in British Columbia, Canada. One of the richest ecosystems in the country, it is also one of the most endangered. At least 118 species of plants, mammals, reptiles, birds, butterflies, dragonflies and other insects are at risk of extinction. The team was formed in 1999 as a comprehensive partnership of experts affiliated with all levels of government, non-governmental organizations, First Nations, and academic institutions. To learn about opportunities for volunteers visit their website at: http://www.goert.ca/

- **The Land Conservancy - British Columbia (TLC)**
  Usually known as "TLC," The Land Conservancy is a nonprofit, charitable land trust that works throughout British Columbia. TLC protects important habitats for native plants and animals as well as properties with historical, cultural, scientific, or compatible recreational value. For information regarding volunteer opportunities (the true lifeblood of the organization) call their volunteer coordinator at (250) 479-8399 or visit their website at: http://www.conservancy.bc.ca/

- **Habitat Acquisition Trust - British Columbia (HAT)**
  HAT is a nonprofit, regional land trust whose mission is to conserve natural environments on southern Vancouver Island and the southern Gulf Islands. HAT accepts donations of property, purchases land, and helps landowners establish permanent legal restrictions to protect natural habitats. For more information call (250) 995-2428 or visit their webpage at: http://www.hat.bc.ca

# Further Reading

There are not many books about the nature of the San Juan Islands that I can recommend to the curious reader. A few of the older works listed here, however, are very good and can be thought of as "classics."

Adams, Evelyn. 1995. *San Juan Islands Wildlife*.
    Seattle: The Mountaineers.

Atkinson, Scott and Fred Sharpe. 1985. *Wild Plants of the San Juan Islands.*
    Seattle: The Mountaineers.

Kozloff, Eugene N. 1983. *Seashore Life of the Northern Pacific Coast*.
    Seattle: University of Washington Press.

Lamb, Andy and Bernard P. Hanby. 2005. *Marine Life of the Pacific Northwest*.
    Madeira Park, B.C.: Harbour Publishing.

Lewis, Mark and Fred Sharpe. 1987. *Birds of the San Juan Islands.*
    Seattle: The Mountaineers.

Mueller, Marge & Ted. 2003 (1979). *The San Juan Islands: Afoot and Afloat*.
    Seattle: The Mountaineers.

Wilcox, Ken. 2001. *Hiking the San Juan Islands*.
    Bellingham, Washington: Northwest Wild Books.

Wortman, Dave. 2005. *San Juan Islands: A Guide to Exploring the Great Outdoors*.
    Guilford, Connecticut: Globe Pequot Press.

Yates, Steve. 1998 (1988). *Marine Wildlife of Puget Sound, the San Juans, and Strait of Georgia*. Seattle: Sasquatch Books.

Yates, Steve. 1992. *Orcas, Eagles & Kings* (The Natural History of Puget Sound and Georgia Strait).
    Primavera Press (Turtleback Books: Friday Harbor, Washington).

# Glossary of Selected Terms

**Bioaccumulation** = occurs when an organism absorbs a toxic substance at a rate greater than that at which the substance is lost. This process becomes more pronounced at every level of predation.

**Controlled burn** = fire is a natural part of both forest and grassland ecology. Prescribed or controlled burning is a technique used in prairie restoration and certain types of forest management.

**Cross-bedding** = refers to inclined sedimentary structures in a horizontal unit of rock that can form in environments where water or wind flows and sand or gravel occur on the bed of the system. Separation of heavy minerals, and changes in flow cycles cause the different planes.

**Ecotone** = a transition zone separating two ecological communities.

**Endemic** = an organism being "*endemic*" means it is exclusively native to a place or biota.

**Estuary** = a semi-enclosed coastal body of water with one or more rivers or streams flowing into it, and with a free connection to the open sea. Estuaries often have high rates of biological productivity.

**Eutrophic** = an ecosystem, usually aquatic, that becomes overly rich with unused nutrients.

**Forb** = a flowering plant with a non-woody stem that is *not* a grass.

**Glacial striations** = scratches or gouges cut into the bedrock by the abrasive process of glacial movement. Striations usually occur as multiple straight, parallel lines scratched by the movement of the sediment-loaded base of the glacier.

**Glacial till** = the unsorted sediment deposited by a glacier. It may vary from clay to mixtures of clay, sand, gravel, and even boulders.

**Honeycomb weathering** = an erosion process in sandstone that creates numerous small cavities that when seen together appear to form a honeycomb pattern.

**Igneous rock** = rock formed from cooled and solidified magma, either below the earth's surface as intrusive (plutonic) rock or on the surface as extrusive (volcanic) rock.

**Midden** = word used by archaeologists to describe any kind of feature containing waste products relating to day-to-day human life.

**Old growth** = sometimes called climax forest, ancient forest, virgin forest, or primary forest. It is an area of forest that has attained great age and often represents the final stage of successionary plant growth. Old growth forests typically contain multiple vertical layers of vegetation of many species, and a mosaic of large live trees and dead trees called "snags."

**Refugia** = locations of isolated or relict populations of once widespread animal or plant species.

**Riparian zone** = the interface between land and a flowing body of surface water. Plant communities along river margins are often called riparian vegetation.

**Savannah** = a woodland ecosystem characterized by trees that are sufficiently small or widely spaced so that the canopy does not close. Most savannahs support an understory of grassland and forbs.

**Sphagnum bog** = also known as a "peat bog." *Sphagnum* is a genus of some 350 species of mosses, collectively known as "peat moss."

# Index

## *Meet the Author*

Terry Domico is well known for his regional ecological assessment work for the conservation and enhancement of critical native plant and wildlife habitats. His articles and photographs have appeared nationally in *Natural History*, *Smithsonian*, *National Wildlife*, and other magazines, and in publications by the National Geographic Society.

*Photo by Jim Maya*

He is also the author of several other books about nature including <u>*WILD HARVEST*</u>, the internationally acclaimed <u>*BEARS OF THE WORLD*</u>, <u>*KANGAROOS: The Marvelous Mob*</u>, <u>*THE LAST THYLACINE*</u>, and was photographer of <u>*THE NATURE OF BORNEO*</u>.

For more than 30 years (when not exploring Asia's vanishing rain forest or the Australian outback) Terry has made his home in the San Juan Islands. You can write to him via e-mail at: *biosurvey@mail.com*